SPARK

# SPARK

*Take Your Business
From Struggle to*
SIGNIFICANCE

DAVID A. HILTON

WITH

Alexander Hilton

New York

# SPARK

*Take Your Business From Struggle to* SIGNIFICANCE

© 2017 DAVID A. HILTON .

Published in New York, New York, by Morgan James Publishing. Morgan James and The Entrepreneurial Publisher are trademarks of Morgan James, LLC.
www.MorganJamesPublishing.com

The Morgan James Speakers Group can bring authors to your live event. For more information or to book an event visit The Morgan James Speakers Group at www.TheMorganJamesSpeakersGroup.com.

**Shelfie**

A **free** eBook edition is available
with the purchase of this print book.

CLEARLY PRINT YOUR NAME ABOVE IN UPPER CASE

**Instructions to claim your free eBook edition:**
1. Download the Shelfie app for Android or iOS
2. Write your name in **UPPER CASE** above
3. Use the Shelfie app to submit a photo
4. Download your eBook to any device

ISBN 978-1-63047-947-3 paperback
ISBN 978-1-63047-948-0 eBook
ISBN 978-1-63047-949-7 hardcover
Library of Congress Control Number:
2016900798

**Cover Design by:**
Rachel Lopez
www.r2cdesign.com

**Interior Design by:**
Bonnie Bushman
The Whole Caboodle Graphic Design

11/14

In an effort to support local communities and raise awareness and funds, Morgan James Publishing donates a percentage of all book sales for the life of each book to Habitat for Humanity Peninsula and Greater Williamsburg.

Get involved today, visit
www.MorganJamesBuilds.com

# DEDICATION

To you, the reader, the person who owns a small to medium-sized business, and to all the clients and team members in my businesses, you have inspired me to find the answers to all your questions about how to build a successful business. You will find many of those answers in this book. I respect and admire your drive to create the American dream for yourselves!

To my son, Alex, who wove these answers along with my business teachings into the story of Jack's journey, you are an amazing person.

To my wife, Suzanne Dolphin, who has supported my work both as my life and business partner—you continue to make my life both rewarding and enjoyable.

# TABLE OF CONTENTS

# ONLINE RESOURCES

To download a study guide and additional resources, please visit:
**www.MySparkBook.com/resources**

Foreword
# START-UP TO
# SMALL BUSINESS

Have you ever dreamed of running your own business? Have you ever been so inspired by your vision of your own business that you want to drop everything and launch your own business? Or are you running your own business and wondering how to grow it to the next level? If so, this book was written especially for you.

When running a business, it is easy to get caught up in the details of today's problems and to lose sight of the larger picture. In addition to providing approaches that can be used to solve today's problems, this book will pull you out of the details and enable you to see the business journey from a higher perspective—a perspective that shows you where you are in the journey of the business. You will see that the challenges are just that: challenges, not insurmountable problems.

As the founder of a business that is going from start-up to rapid growth, I found this book to contain a wealth of knowledge that not only answered many questions but also gave me a longer-term perspective on what to expect. I found myself relating at a visceral level to Jack's experience of launching his business. I saw myself in his experiences—I felt his enthusiasm and inspiration as he started to make his vision a reality, the weight of reality as he struggled to get the business off the ground, and his joy and confidence as the business reached stability and success.

I felt the same inspiration and sense of disbelief as I launched my business. Like Jack, I was off to make my dream a reality. The gulp that Jack felt as he answered the phone for the first time, announcing "Jack's Modern Design," was the same I felt as I spoke to my first clients. A dream come true—perhaps too good to be true.

People often have a passion for something and launch a business so that they can live that passion. This was the case for Jack, and it was the case for me with my love of capturing timeless emotion and family connections in heirloom portrait art pieces. Jack's reality check—how hard he had to work for less money in the beginning to get his business off the ground, and how much work was involved that was unrelated to his passion—evoked the feelings I had had after I launched my business. After the excitement of taking action to live the dream, the dust settled and reality set in. There is a lot more to running a business than merely the passion that drove us to it.

As hard as the weight and reality of this realization hit Jack, it hit me, and I felt his distress at a gut level. It was a hard realization that our businesses, born of our passion, required much more than the ability to do what we love to do. Once Vern helped Jack see that this realization was a natural part of the journey and that he could take control of his destiny, create the business of his dreams and get through to the other side by putting a goal and plan in place, it all seemed manageable again. If you, like Jack, have begun to lose your energy, you will feel your energy and inspiration return as you take control of your business and put your plans and goals in place.

Watching Jack navigate the relationships among his employees and the different styles that his employees had for managing problems and conflict was painful. It was a relief when Vern stepped in to offer the communications and management strategies that allowed Jack to help his employees understand how to work together and what the rules were. With this clarity, Jack began putting a communications and management structure in place that would not only make his employees feel more comfortable but also dramatically increase their performance and the performance of the business. Vern's lesson was, once again, about the leader of the business taking charge of the business and being accountable for its performance. This lesson made me sit back and contemplate the culture I am creating and how to make my business a great place to work.

I felt, at a visceral level, the dread and fear that Jack felt at that moment he was about to lose his business due to what he saw was a significant mistake. It was the sort of mistake that we all could imagine happening to ourselves with financial consequences that seem too large to overcome for a fledgling business. By unleashing his creativity and determination and controlling his fear and anxiety, he was able to work through the situation and recover from the disaster. It was a great reminder that obstacles that feel insurmountable are a natural course of business, and they can be overcome.

This book is a combination of a fast-paced novel with powerful, impactful and eminently executable business lessons. As I read this book for the first time, I started to take notes but then became engrossed with Jack's journey and read the book as a novel. The second time I read it as a business book and took notes on business lessons, approaches, and solutions. It is rare to find a business book that is enjoyable to read while being power packed full of knowledge.

As an entrepreneur will be able to relate to this story and its lessons, if you follow the approach and insights given, you will have the tools at your fingertips to run your business very, very successfully. Put the knowledge into action and then, like me, you will see the results.

Where Jack had Vern, I am fortunate to have the opportunity to work with David Hilton, a highly knowledgeable, successful, and rigorous business coach who has helped me see the road ahead, put the plan into place, and then execute the plan. He often says that he is the taillights in the fog. It is up to me to drive, but he will me show the way. And he does. Every time.

**—Lili Engelhardt**
Chapel Hill, NC

An entrepreneur with a successful track record, Lili Engelhardt, MBA, has used the principles laid out in this book to increase her current business by over 400% in the last year.

# ENTREPRENEUR TO MEDIUM-SIZE BUSINESS

You may be wondering what you can get from this book and how to interpret what it says. Maybe you are even wondering whether if you went to a prestigious business school, they would give you the same advice. No, they wouldn't. They would tell you what a business looks like from the outside, as they study it. You and I, on the other hand, are on the inside. We need insight about which things to do next, not data about the consequences of having done them.

You are probably here because you want your business to grow, and you don't want to pay the price of reinventing the wheel. Sound like what you're thinking? Good. You are in the right place. (Even if you don't want to improve your business, this is a great story. Read it just as a novel.)

I remember the early days of my business… Some scars will be with me forever. I'm talking about the days before I knew how to do what I was actually in the middle of doing. The days before I knew what would work and what wouldn't, or when I didn't know how to do what I needed to get done… (And, more importantly, what not to do.)

My first "real" business (real means having at least: more than one customer, letterhead, regular expenses, etc.) was founded when I was only 13 years old. A buddy of mine and I did radio and TV repair for a couple of years—back when you could actually fix electronics. Mostly this business taught me how much I didn't know. It never made any money. And, needless to say, it didn't last.

Do you know that most new businesses fail with two years? The electronics repair shop was right in that window, for the same reasons as every other business that crashes. We didn't know what we needed to know. Vision and desire alone are not enough. We didn't know how to manage—or what to manage. And, we sure didn't know how to run a business. Energy and desire are required for success, *and* alone they cannot overcome ignorance and limited common sense. You need to know the right things to do.

Time goes by, and from the foundations you uncover from trial and error plus sage advice from people like David, you go on to build successful, durable businesses that may go onto to be a recognized leader in your space. The essential ingredients for this success are: being entrepreneurial (accepting the risk, being forceful) and continuing to learn and grow over time. An MBA is not required.

This book tells the story of the journey that gets you from here to there. From an idea to execution. It points out, in context, the lessons that everyone who wants to be successful in business must learn. Using the information in this book, *you* can learn and grow in the comfort of your living room where there is no cost to changing your mind or making a mistake. (Whereas, the authors and I made many of our mistakes in the real world and paid for them in cash. I have made at least one million dollar mistake.)

Don't think this is just about small businesses. Small businesses are what drives our economy. The majority of businesses in America are small businesses—fewer than ten employees and less than $2 million in annual revenue. But even the largest business was a small startup on its first day. (Apple Computer lived for months in a garage.) Since all businesses are small at some point, the story is cast from this perspective. The lessons here are appropriate for a startup or smaller business. And, the story doesn't change for a larger business. In fact, I used these same principles to build a high-tech business that, in under ten years, became Microsoft's Partner of the Year Worldwide, sold its consulting division to a major Industry player and then sold its training division to a local college. Tens of millions of dollars in value (back when a million dollars was real money) and hundreds of jobs were created in a very short time—without millions in venture capital—just hard work and focus.

The only thing that may be different between us is the marketplace in which you choose to play and your vision within that space. Our vision was to be technology evangelists, and we wanted to change the world. And we did. (The World Economic Forum recognized us as Technology Pioneers.) But the way you build a business, the way you execute day-to-day is the same for nearly everyone. Why? Because just as gravity, the speed of light and the laws of physics are the same for all of us, the world of business has essential "laws" as well (finance, taxation, marketing, hiring) that are the same for everyone too.

The purpose of this book is to show you how to navigate these laws of business as you experience them in the real world.

Our hero, Jack, is about to learn all the lessons of business the hard way so that you don't have to. Let's wish him well and watch how he makes out.

—**Bruce Backa**
Nashua, NH

Bruce Backa started his career in big business, having been the Director of Business Research for the American Stock Exchange and CTO of AIG. Since entering the startup world, he has been recognized as a Technology Pioneer by the World Economic Forum and founded a company that Microsoft selected as its Partner of the Year, Worldwide.

# Chapter 1
# THE SPARK

I always wanted to be an architect and design buildings. Heck, I even went to school for it—two years at the University of New Mexico studying architecture. I loved it. I loved everything about it, especially the art and the science of drawing up the schematics and incorporating the latest designs. And, at the end of the day, I liked that each project would stand as an enduring monument to the architect's efforts.

But here I was, working as a carpenter in the middle of a construction zone, on the weekend, sweating from a hard day's work, drained by the oppressive humidity. Here I am, looking up at the steel frame of the office building I had been hired to help put together for some booming IT firm created by a bunch of MIT students, who had gotten together and created the "latest and greatest" social network that had gone viral overnight. They were now expanding and centralizing their offices in this quiet Boston suburb. Looking at the project, I thought about how the fruits of my labor would appear on the outside: a giant black monolith looking like it came straight from 2001: A Space Odyssey. I sighed—for a group of visionaries they sure had no taste. Couldn't they have chosen something a bit more creative?

My dream of becoming an architect had been sidelined the day my father got hit in a drunk-driving accident. In different ways, the accident devastated both my father and my mother. My father, who became disabled and never fully regained his old self, had been a lobsterman, a hard laborer who believed in working for every dime. My mother, an art historian, could not earn enough for the family with part-time adjunct work, so she took on a job as a local sales clerk to help out. She did her best to make my father happy every day. They have been married thirty-five years, and their relationship—one of the most amazing I had ever witnessed—had been sorely tested.

To help support the family, I dropped out of architecture school. I chose to get into the closest thing to architecture I could: carpentry. Mastering this trade would require another few years of expensive tuition bills, but at least, I'd get paid during my apprenticeship. And better yet, I knew, from the beginning, I would be good at it. Sure, I wouldn't be designing buildings myself, but I was good enough to give some insight to the architects I worked with. I guess what it takes to build something and having a final vision in mind helped me the most. Sometimes, like on this project, carpentry was hard, boring work. But at least, it paid the bills, right?

Driving home at the end of the day, I thought about my chosen career. Even though I was making enough money to put food on the table and take a couple of weekend trips to New Hampshire each year, and even though Erica and I lived a peaceful life and had considered having kids (still concerned about the costs, though), I worried what would happen to my future family if, like my father, I became incapacitated. Would my children be secure and well provided for? Would they be happy?

A chill shot up my spine—such a chill that I drove straight past my exit. A chill in the form of the question, "Am I really happy?"

I didn't know if the question had ever crossed my mind. It was so daunting I didn't even know how to approach it. Was I content? Yes. I had a loving wife and a good, stable job. Sure I could use a few more vacations and maybe a higher salary, but that could come with a promotion.

I laughed. A *promotion?* The only promotion I'd be up for was to be a site manager, and my company, Gregory's Building and Housing (or GBH as we called it), almost uniformly required an MBA for that role. There's no way I could take time off to get that, let alone pay the tuition for grad school.

I pulled into my driveway. That shocker chill had been replaced by a sinking feeling. I put the car in park and pressed my forehead into the top of the steering wheel. *Is my career a dead end?*

"Bah," I said to myself. "There are a few managers at GBH, who don't have an MBA. All I need to do is show them my ideas. I did well in school for architecture. I'm sure I can contribute and get promoted." A timid smile crept over my face. I knew it was a long shot, but maybe I wasn't in a dead end job after all. Maybe I could be among those few.

"Jack, you're late!" Erica called out. "Did you get stuck in traffic?"

I looked at my watch; it was almost a quarter of an hour later than I said I would be home. After taking off my boots and leaving them at the entrance, I walked down the hallway, drawn by the wafting aroma of a Montreal-seasoned steak with rice pilaf and balsamic asparagus. In the kitchen, Erica turned to me and smiled.

At a little over five feet tall, Erica was a foot shorter than me. But, what she may have lacked in size, she made up for in spirit. She had been a florist since she was eighteen. She loved flowers and enjoyed their beauty. She had a love for all life—in fact, we met when we were both volunteering at the animal shelter down the road. We had much in common and immediately hit it off. Both of us were tied down by family situations; Erica had been going to college when her mother needed surgery, and she had to leave school to care for her. But Erica always said that as long as she had the "simple things in life," as she called them, she was happy. Coming home to her helped me make it through every week. She spread positivity—and tonight, I needed it.

"Happy birthday!" she squealed as she ran over and hugged me. Her embrace made it seem like everything was all right.

I looked at the steak sizzling on the skillet and the asparagus in the pan. Their aromas banished the uneasiness I had felt.

Later, as we lay in bed, facing each other, I told her about my concerns for a promotion and making my college dreams a reality.

"You have great ideas!" she responded. "You just never share them with others unless asked. You know a lot of things, and they have listened to your ideas in the past; maybe you just need to put them in front of management more often."

I thought about what she said and vowed that the very next day I would try to get management's ear a bit more. As I drifted to sleep, I felt content. I had a plan. I would make the best of the next decade of my life.

The next morning, after my alarm had roused me from a deep sleep, I slowly made my way down the staircase to the kitchen, where I turned on the coffee machine. I sat down at the counter to wait for the coffee to brew. I thought about my new commitment. I didn't know why I never thought about it in the past, but even as a carpenter I could include design plans. I chuckled, and said to myself, "How hard would it be to install modern tech into the building we are working on?" It seemed plain as day; maybe all we'd have to do is ask our customers if they would want that sort of stuff. I contemplated a few ideas. Rick, my manager, would be in today. I would let him know my thoughts. We had a good working relation, and he frequently asked me for my suggestions. This time, though, I was going to approach him first.

I grabbed my coffee and stepped into my boots. In the car, I smiled, *How long has it been since I felt excited to go to work?* As I drove to the project site, I thought about how I would approach Rick.

Pulling into the office parking lot, I saw Rick's sleek black Cadillac, my stomach jumped; there was no getting out of this. Part of me was hoping I wouldn't have to present my ideas to my boss; what if he shot them down? "No," I muttered under my breath, "This has to work."

I walked into the complex. As I made my way to the fifth floor, I noticed the men putting up the girders, setting up the flooring, and laying out the indents that the wiring would travel. In its skeletal form, the building was beautiful. However, once it was enclosed, according to its present plans, there would be nothing comparable visually. It would be a plain black monolith.

I saw Rick. He was looking over the construction, shouting out the occasional compliment to each of the other carpenters on the floor: "Hey Bill, good job on that framework! Think you can get it done by five today?" I went over to him. Noticing me, he turned and yelled out over the noise, "Jack! How are you? I saw what you did last night, brilliant work!" I signaled that I wanted to chat with him in private. He yelled out to the crew, "Keep it up everyone!" before indicating that we should go downstairs.

The quiver in the pit of my stomach had returned, but I took a deep breath and pushed the feeling aside. Away from the screech and roar of the equipment, Rick repeated himself: "As I said, brilliant work last night. To be honest, I didn't believe you when you said you'd be done by seven!"

Good old Rick, I thought. He always knew how to make his staff feel accepted. He did his best to keep us in a positive mood. I had seen him come down hard on a couple of the crew before, but when he did it seemed to devastate him too.

Even though my stomach seemed OK, now I had a lump in my throat. "Rick," I said, "I was wondering, given that this is an IT building, shouldn't we be including some, I don't know, some actual technology in this building?"

Rick looked a little perplexed.

"I mean," I continued, "it just seems that this building is, well, mundane, and it's been bothering me. It is like the architect doesn't know what could potentially be included. This building could symbolize the future of architecture!"

Rick laughed. I gulped. He sat down on a nearby sawhorse and said, "OK, I'll bite. What do you mean?"

I started talking, rambling even, about things I learned in school, about technologies that had developed in the past decade, things I believed every building should have. "Why should people have to get up and turn on the lights when they can just give a simple verbal command to turn them on or off? Why should the security system have codes the employees have to memorize when they could just hold their hand up to a scanner? Why should—"

Rick held up his hand. "Jack, I admit I sometimes wonder the same thing. And you know it would be great if every building worked like that. But that's just not what we do. Those MIT grads, with all their online connections, hired us for one simple thing: to build this building. Sure, it's not a glamorous building. Hell, I'd say it's among the most generic buildings we've ever built." He paused and looked me in the eye. "Jack, I know you wanted to become an architect, but that isn't what you are here for. You are a great carpenter, and more than that, you have insight into your projects. I've directed some of our contractors to approach you and ask for your advice on some things. For example, your idea of an open glass ceiling at the Vernon Welsh

Library was brilliant! But sometimes our job is just to do exactly what we are asked, and only that."

I stared at my feet. I knew he was right. I was just another worker on a project. I looked up at him, "Do you think the designer even *knows* about this building's potential?"

Rick hesitated before answering. "Hmm, as far as I know, he doesn't. He is some kid fresh out of MIT, who's a friend of the owner. But, Jack, it is not our job to ask or even tell them. They're asking for a simple job, and they're paying. So we'll give it to them."

On that day, we were working on the wall structures. As I was laying the foundation, I couldn't get what Rick had said out of my head: "He doesn't know." What if he did? What if someone told the design team how to improve their ideas? What if they knew what they could get? As questions flooded my mind, I could barely focus on my work.

After I had clocked out for the day, I raced to my car. I was jittery with excitement and just wanted to speed home. I turned on the radio. "I need to find out!" I yelled above a blaring rock song. It just didn't make sense to me that our firm wouldn't try to upsell them. Sure, we focus on delivering quickly and at a relatively low price, but adding some additional features wouldn't take all that long, and people pay a fortune for them.

I pulled into the driveway and rushed into the house. As the computer booted up, I stared at the flickering lights. It seemed an infinitely slow metronome. *Hurry up. Let me at my research!* Soon I had opened almost twenty windows, everyone a link leading to a new idea—nothing I hadn't seen in the past, but now they had new meaning. Clearly there was a market: in-home theaters, integrated security, intercoms throughout buildings that could play music, and solar panels that could be built into the roof to look natural to the building.

So many ideas. So simple to do. *I can do this!*

I stormed downstairs yelling, "Erica! Erica!" I found a note on the kitchen counter: "Gone grocery shopping, back at 6:30." *A half-hour from now.* I couldn't contain myself!

*This is what I have always wanted to do*, I thought. Finally, a means to do architecture and structure it around what I knew best. I imagined the kinds of projects I could do, like walls that have touch panels instead of light switches, or that you control by just saying "lights on" or "lights off."

To do it my way, all I would have to do is start my own business. But I couldn't even get a management position. But then again, people started businesses all the time. How hard could it be?

My runaway train of thought was broken by the sound of Erica coming in. Even before she had a chance to say, "Honey I'm home," I was at the door. I took one of the grocery bags from her.

"OK, what happened?" she said.

I tilted my head to look at her "Nothing, hon. I just had a wonderful idea."

She smiled. "Well, let's get the groceries into the kitchen and we can talk about it while I put them away."

I made two trips to the car while Erica unpacked the bags. Once we had everything in, she asked, "So what is this wonderful idea of yours? Planning on building us a pool?"

I laughed. In the past, I had done some remodeling on the house just for fun, and she always wanted a pool. "No, no, no. I want to build a *business*."

"What?" she gagged, just about dropping a package of vegetables.

"I have put a lot of thought into it, and I think I have a brilliant idea that we could build a business around."

"OK, let's hear it."

I started telling her about the research I had done, about my ideas, about how I could actually become what I've always wanted to become and be using the knowledge I already had. "I can think like a carpenter and design like an architect, and there's a huge market of people wanting custom designs and features. I know I can do it. It is what I have always dreamed about."

She looked up at the ceiling as if lost in thought. I waited for what seemed like an eternity. Finally, she looked down at her feet and spoke. "I would never want to hold you back from your dream," she said solemnly, "but it seems like there are a lot of risks. You'd have to quit your job if you did this." She sighed deeply. "I'll tell you what: you figure out what it takes to open a business and how to work it and make double sure you can do everything it takes, and I'll support you one hundred percent, no questions asked. Just please, please, please do lots of research."

I thought my heart skipped a beat. With Erica's support, my dream finally seemed within reach. I felt like I glided across the tile floor when I stepped over to hug her. We both smiled. I slept deeply that night, and the next morning even woke up with a smile. All I needed to do now was some research.

During my lunch break, I looked online for the "how to" books I might need. After reading a few articles, I ordered a few no-brainer guides to business and taxation and a book about business startup and development. I figured the last one, at least, would make for some light reading.

When the package of books arrived a few days later, I could barely contain myself. I rushed into the house and tore it open like a child opening his Christmas presents.

Over the next week, I immersed myself in licensing, taxation, and accounting. With my brain reeling, it was time to give myself a small break. So what about the business development book? I looked over the cover and flipped through a couple of pages. Nothing about it grabbed my attention, so I couldn't tell if reading it would be worth my time. I put it on the kitchen counter for later; maybe I would pick it up another time when I was bored.

That night, Erica went to bed early. Nothing on the television interested me, so I just left the channel on the news and turned down the volume. For the umpteenth time, I reviewed my notes and plans about the business. When I went to the fridge for a snack, I noticed the business development book still on the counter, so I took it with me back to the couch.

It started out with some psychological mumbo-jumbo about the mindset of an entrepreneur. An easy read, I thought, it's nine now, I'll go to bed by ten. By ten, I had changed my attitude. The book talked about what drove people to start small businesses—people just like me. I whispered to myself, "Doesn't it always feel that way." Little quotes like "Don't be afraid to dream" peppered the text and flew off the pages at me as they rang true.

"Many people are 'dreamers,'" read one passage. "Many more are 'doers.' But it is only the relative few individuals who can combine their dreams with systems needed to execute them that find true success." I sighed, I wanted to succeed, I wanted my dream to become a reality, and I wanted to do anything and everything it took for that dream to become a reality. I kept reading, drawn more and more deeply into the stories in the book. They were about mindset, and, unlike the other books, they were about what I must do every day to truly turn my architectural fantasy into reality.

One chapter was entitled "Self-Discipline and Success." A passage read, "Self-discipline gives you the ability to turn raw potential into success. Self-discipline allows you to convert your gifts and your experience into action. Self-discipline keeps you on track and allows you to follow through on your plans." I paused and said to myself, "I must have self-discipline if I'm going to turn my gifts into action." The book continued with three plans to boost my self-discipline:

1. Conquer your least appealing tasks first thing in the morning.
2. Shore up your weaknesses, one at a time, so that they don't hold you back.
3. Be accountable for your actions, set goals, and share them with your peers.

I pulled out my notepad. I had never thought about this. Once I was up and running with the business, maybe I should balance the books in the morning; maybe I should shore up on making contacts; maybe I should discuss with Erica each step of the business. It seemed so easy, yet so real.

As I kept reading, almost every word resonated with me, and finally, I came to the secrets of a successful business owner: *strategic vision.*

- The ability to combine vision with action.
- The ability to set (and track) specific goals.
- The ability to communicate proactively.
- The ability to learn from mistakes, rather than be defeated by them.
- The ability to inspire others.

I jotted down how I stood with each secret:

I had combined vision with action.

I was setting specific goals.

Communications and inspiration, I supposed, would come later.

Hopefully, I would never have to learn from mistakes—or at least not giant ones.

I knew I was on the right track. All I had to do was implement the tools and start a business, and then just keep these points in mind. It seemed all too easy. I glanced at the clock. It was 11:30! I was hardly through the first few chapters! I slapped the book closed. I had to go to bed, or I would sleep straight through my alarm. Everything seemed so clear. Starting a business would just take a bit of paper pushing combined with the concept of strategic vision in the business development book—and I was already on track with that, or so I thought. I just needed to get my ducks in order, and I could do this—I could make my dream a reality. Soon, I would be the architect, the designer, and the builder of my destiny.

After setting the book on my nightstand, to avoid waking Erica, I carefully crawled into bed, then lay down and slowly drifted to sleep.

## Chapter 2
# FRIENDS OF OLD

‐‐‐‐‐‐‐‐‐‐‐‐‐‐‐‐‐‐‐‐‐‐‐‐

Time flew by, and month after month passed as I made my plans.

I didn't even have a name for my dream business. How could I start it without a name? For weeks it seemed like every few seconds I would pull a small notepad from my pocket and jot down a name. Finally, I settled with "Jack's Modern Design." It wasn't the most creative name, but it seemed perfect for what I wanted to do.

Now, for a loan.

Unless I wanted to sink my entire retirement into this dream idea, I would need a loan. The bank offered $25,000, but only once I was incorporated. I had hoped for more because $25,000 barely covered tools, materials, and a truck. I would have to front most of the money after all.

While I filled in and filed forms, I was also calling up old contacts. Getting incorporated just took paperwork; getting actual *jobs* was a whole other monster. My old contacts were a mishmash of real estate developers and building designers. They said they found my business idea interesting, but all their jobs were already in the works. They said they'd call back, not that I believed it.

Meanwhile at the GBH site, we were starting work on the final floor of the black monolith. With the lower level windows already in, entering it felt like going into a tomb. How fitting. If I couldn't get work for my business, how would I be able to leave this place? As I started laying the floor base at the top level, I heard a voice shout, "Jack!" Looking up, I saw Dan waving at me. He came over. "Jack, it seems like we haven't seen you in months. Say—we're going out later tonight. There's a little pub just a few blocks from here. You should join us."

I didn't want to. I was worried that after all my effort, nothing seemed to be panning out. "I don't know, Dan. I was planning on spending the night with the wife."

Dan laughed and slapped me on the back. "Hah. See you at six." He never took "no" for an answer. I went back to my work.

The next thing I noticed was the distant ringing of a church bell. Six clangs. I had worked late again. As I was exiting the IT mausoleum, I heard laughter. It was Dan and a few others. "Working late again, Jack?" Bill said.

"Oh, you know me. I always get too absorbed with my work."

They laughed.

"Seeing how long it's been since we last hung out, I was worried they had you building the whole thing!" Dan exclaimed.

The guys were right. I hadn't been as social as I could be, and they'd been good to me. I guess I was ready for a break with my friends.

At the pub, we pulled a couple of tables together while Dan went to the counter and ordered for us. Returning to the table, he asked me, "So, Jack, where have you been all this time?"

I stared down at the table for a moment. I felt like I no longer fit in, like I had gotten so wrapped up in working on my dream, I had alienated myself from my friends. Looking back up, though, I saw they were genuinely concerned and interested. "I've started a business," I told them.

"Really?" Bill said. "You know, I considered doing that once. I figured I could make some money on side jobs, a few extra contracts here or there. I never got the idea off the ground, though."

"Yeah, well, mine's not totally off the ground yet either," I said. I told them what happened, that I incorporated, set up a bank loan, but wasn't going to do anything until I got my first contract.

They all chortled. John went into a rant about my having a stable job right now and about how I'd be throwing away a good career. Some of them nodded their heads in agreement.

I told them that I understood and that if things didn't pan out, I would probably continue to work with Gregory's Building and Housing. Soon the conversation turned to what was happening in everyone's home life and Sunday sports. But, their few comments got me worried. *Could they be right? Could this be a wasted endeavor?*

At eight o'clock we headed back to the construction site and our cars. One of the men grabbed me from behind. It was Mark.

"Jack," Mark whispered, "I thought about what you said, about having trouble getting your first contract. Well, my brother forwarded me a contact. Some upscale realtor across town is building a bunch of fancy houses. I don't know the project details, but I'm too busy at home to take it." He handed me the realtor's business card and continued. "Besides, if things don't pan out, I'm sure Rick would hire you back."

I settled into the Nissan and stared at the beat-up business card I held in my hand. *My first lead. What do I do? Send an email? Call? Send up a smoke signal?* I was nervous and excited at the same time. I wanted to pull out my phone and call the number right then. As I drove home, though, a fog of doubt rolled into my mind: *What if I couldn't do it?*

That night I couldn't sleep. I listened to the clock ticking for what seemed like hours. The fog hung over me. I got up and went to the study and turned on the radio. I wondered if my fear of failure was holding me back. An image of Yoda, from *Star Wars*, popped into my mind. I remembered his words: "Try not. Do or do not—there is no 'try.'" I laughed at myself. *Great—now I'm taking advice from a sci-fi movie!*

I went into the bathroom and looked in the mirror. I wasn't sure what I saw in that drawn and exhausted-looking reflection, but I had to ask, *who was I?* Then I realized that was the wrong question. Rather, I needed to ask, *who do I want to be?* I returned to the study, grabbed a notepad, and started to write.

I've created this business, so I'm going stick with it. Why should I close up shop before I have even opened? If things don't pan out with this contact, maybe the next one will. I wrote down an alternative plan, other ideas, and what made my business idea unique. I searched the internet for a few ideas and bumped into a quote from Henry Ford: "If I had asked people what they wanted, they would have asked for faster horses." Isn't that what it was all about? Innovation?

As I wrote, the fog of doubt lifted. Getting through it, to visualize success was one of the most difficult things I had done in my life.

I woke up late the next morning—fortunately, it was my day off. I went downstairs to grab my morning cup of coffee. When I saw the crumpled business card lying by the phone, my heart began to pound. I picked up the phone and dialed the number.

A woman answer with an abrupt, "Mornin', this is Cowen Realtors, Shannon speaking. How can I help you?"

"Hello Shannon, this is Jack, from Jack's Modern Design." I paused before pushing through my racing thoughts and the lump in my throat. "I heard you needed a carpenter for one of your housing projects."

"One moment, sir." I started to sweat as I heard the clicking and clacking of a keyboard. "Hold on, I'm transferring your call." The phone began to ring again. A gruff voice came on, "Hello, Dave Cowen."

"Hi, Mr. Cowen, this is Jack from Jack's Modern Design. I heard you were in need of a carpenter for a housing project."

I heard a cough. "Ah, yes, you mean the project up on Mallord Street. We've got a few rooms that need some specialization, very high-tech in-home theaters. We got the electronics and materials for it but are having trouble finding a carpenter with experience with this stuff. How about we meet later? I have got some time at around three today. Can you be up by Mallord at that time?"

My stress dropped away as I said, "Sure thing. I'll be there at three." We hung up. *Yes! Jack's Modern Design exists!*

At fifteen minutes before three, driving up Mallord Street I saw seven homes under construction. Each home looked like a near bare frame with just a few walls and windows set up. The structures were beautiful. Each home seemed to be built around a giant circle. Each had a circular deck cropping out to one side and branches off the house that rose up like towers from a castle.

I parked my car and strolled around. The first and most complete house I walked up to was three stories tall. The basement was built into the hillside, where what looked like giant bay windows opened up into an unfinished concrete base. This must be where the home theater would be. I walked down and looked at the view from windows. It was an amazing vista overlooking the town.

Hearing an approaching vehicle, I walked back up the hillside. A silver BMW drove up and parked behind my Nissan. A tall, gaunt man wearing a blue suit and tie got out. He must have been four inches taller than me. He approached me and said, "Greetings, Jack. I'm Dave Cowen. So how do you like what you see?"

"The houses are gorgeous," I said, "but the site seems quiet. I expected workmen to be around here."

"Some new town zoning ordinance has created a delay," replied Cowen. "Our lawyers worked it out, but we've paused construction for the next few weeks."

Perfect, I thought—I can give Rick my two-week notice and leave on friendly terms.

"Let me show you what we've got," said Cowen. We walked back down the hill toward the basement of the house I had been looking at. "Originally this was going to be a day room—thus the massive space for a bay window—but then some of our prospects wanted to have a home theater. The windows let in too much light and would ruin the theater during the day." He paused, and sighed, "The trouble is that we can't rebuild the bay window without rearranging a massive chunk of the upper levels."

I peered into the basement through the window hole to see a giant circular room with a spiral staircase in the far corner. I thought for a second then said, "Maybe we can do both."

"What do you mean?" Cowen asked. I told him about a new shaded glass we could use to turn the windows near black, that swivel chairs could be added to open up the room, and that the projector and the screen could retract into the ceiling.

"You could do that?" he asked.

"Easily—if cost isn't an issue." *Damn*, I thought. *I shouldn't have said that, now he definitely won't hire me for the job.*

Cowen looked up, "If you can run the numbers and give me an estimate, I'll let you know," he replied. "But these are upscale clientele, so you can go wild, within reason of course. Money isn't an issue if the quality is great. And, by the way, you just gave them an extra room, a theater, *and* a day room; I'm surprised you are not an architect."

I contained my enthusiasm. This is what I wanted—my dream was coming to fruition. We talked some more about what had to be done, and he told me to give him a call in twenty days to see when they would start construction again. I was so giddy when I got home that I instantly started running the numbers. Sure, some components would be expensive, but I was finally designing something new, something of my own, and something other people would enjoy. I loved everything about it. Finally, Jack's Modern Design would create things that would last.

I spoke with Cowen a few times after our meeting. He told me that he enjoyed my concept and said that it was feasible for the project. He also said that they might be able to jack up the house prices by almost a hundred grand and that construction would resume in a few weeks. I would be remodeling all seven houses.

I gave my notice at work. Over the next two weeks, I said my farewells. Rick wished me well and hoped the best. I thanked Mark for the connection.

I secured a bank loan for the tools and materials for my start-up. Then I had to sink almost three-quarters of my retirement into the remaining items. Even though Erica was concerned about money, she also noticed this was the happiest I had been since our honeymoon.

On my final day with Gregory's Building and Housing, I looked at the black monolith. Now that I was leaving, the sun's reflection off its black surface made it seem more like a becalmed ocean. On my first morning as a business owner, I hopped out of bed and rushed downstairs. I grabbed my coffee and headed out the door, stopping for a moment to admire my company truck. It was just a simple four-by-four pickup loaded with my tools, but across its side "Jack's Modern Design" was emblazoned in giant black letters underlined in red. Starting it up for its first workday I couldn't help but giggle; for the first time, I was in love with my work.

When I arrived at the Mallord project, a grizzly bear of a man approached me. "You Jack?" he asked. I nodded. "I'm supervising for Mr. Cowen," he said. "Don't worry, I won't get in your way; but just before you move down into the houses let me know. I don't want too many hands in the same spot at the same time." He pointed at the first house. "Your special windows and some other supplies were delivered yesterday. I had them moved to the first floor. Did you bring any additional hands or will you need help moving stuff?"

"Nope, just me. I should be able to do most of it myself, except putting the windows in place."

"All right then, just ask if you need anything. We have roughly three months to get all this done. That damned ordinance set us back, and Mr. Cowen wants to expedite the process. Good luck."

I looked at the house. It seemed to me that three months was easily enough time. I jumped into my work, a smile all over my face. Time flew by faster than it had since my college days, and every day I came home happy.

One day I looked up at the nearly completed first house. The upper floors still needed some work, but the basement was done. I marveled at the work I had accomplished in such a short time. The other homes were nearing completion too: three only needed some electrical work, and three more had a few flooring issues to sort out. Among them, one home still needed the bay window installed. I had about two weeks left, but I was on track. When I got home that day and pulled the mail out of the mailbox, there was a stack of bills. *Uh oh.*

I came in and sat down at the kitchen counter and started opening them. They were all addressed to Jack's Modern Design. The first few were for a hundred or so dollars for miscellaneous items related to work. The bank loan was about a grand. When I started the project, I had received a down payment of twenty-five thousand dollars. I figured paying these bills would be easy, so I put them aside to pay later. Doing the books was really not my thing, and besides, I had to finish my work. I turned in for the night.

The next day I was the first to arrive at the Mallord site. Before anyone else came, I walked around from house to house looking for what I could do next, and I remembered there was one bay window left to install. Even though I knew it wasn't the wisest thing to try to install on my own—each panel of glass was massive, curved to fit the shape of the home, and quite heavy—I chose to do it rather than wait for help. I lifted it and slid it into its frame. I looked around for my drill to lock the frame in place. I saw it on the far side of the room. I carefully balanced the window and left it to get it. Drill now in hand, I turned around and *slam!* All of a sudden I was flat on the floor with an extension cord wrapped around my ankle, my ears ringing.

I lay there and listened—the sound was from outside, not from my ears. I looked up. The window was gone. I hurried to the window frame and looked out: like irregular diamonds, thousands—no, *millions*—of pieces of glass were scattered over the hillside. I swore at myself. *Five grand down the toilet! I knew this could happen! Why was I so stupid?*

That evening I went over the books. Even with the day's incident, it seemed, I was still ahead, especially with the final completion payment of additional fifty grand. However, something felt odd. I started over, crunching the numbers with my calculator. Everything seemed all right. Even after taxes, I came out ahead. But I still felt like I was overlooking something. Then it hit me like a bolt of lightning. I was putting in nearly sixty hours a week, almost fifteen hours a week more than my previous job, and after taxes, per hour, I was making *less than half* what I used to.

I always knew I wouldn't be making as much as before initially, but this? What about the mortgage? What if something happened to me and I couldn't work? The "what-ifs" kept coming. Did I get so caught up in the moment that I didn't even bother to check my take-home? I heard Erica come in. I wanted to tell her, but I was too ashamed. Sure, it seemed like my dream had become reality, but reality seemed to twist my dream yet again.

I didn't know what to do. Again my mind was flooded with questions: Wasn't I doing everything right? Aren't people happy with my work? This is only one setback. Something's wrong, but what? Who can I talk to?

My dreams that night were filled with numbers and people. The numbers were about the half of what I should be making. Half! The people were my wife—who supported me—and those who had warned me.

I woke up feeling groggy after an awful night's sleep. I didn't want to go to work that day.

Like a zombie, I walked to my truck.

For the first time, I hated my work—not just carpentry, but architecture as well. What was the point? It seemed like no matter what I did I ended up at a dead end: a dead-end job, a dead-end business, a dead-end life. Who cared about the art, the science, the making of something that stands and lasts if I can't live well, both at work and at home? I felt destined to always hate my work.

Every second at work felt likes years. I worked slowly and didn't get as much done as I should have. As I got in the truck at the end of the day, I considered not going straight home. I didn't want to face Erica.

I drove aimlessly around town when I saw a small bookshop with a coffee shop inside. On a whim, I stopped and went inside. The scent of the dark roast lifted my spirits. As I drank my brew I couldn't help but ruminate, *what was wrong?*

# Chapter 3
## A WISE MAN AND HARD LESSONS

A s I examined the blackness in my cup with my reflection staring up at me, a man at a table across the room glanced at me over his newspaper. He came over and sat down at my table and started talking. He was an elderly gentleman wearing a suit that matched his gray hair. He wore a pair of the largest glasses I thought I had ever seen. "I haven't seen you in here before," he began, "but you look familiar. Usually, I'm good with faces, and I swear I have seen yours but for the better part of a quarter-hour I've been trying to place you."

I scanned his face. "I don't think we've met. I've been too busy with my business to get out, so unless you are a carpenter I might have bumped into—"

"Ah, so you're a business owner," he interrupted. "Tell me what sort of business is it?"

I couldn't say why, maybe because he seemed friendly, or maybe because I really didn't want to be alone, but once I started talking I couldn't stop. I went into detail about the vision I had when I started the business, the latest project, and about trying to use the most modern ideas in home design.

He listened intently, his eyes shining under his large magnifying glasses. "It sounds intriguing," he said when I had finished. "I have had a few projects done where I swear the architects knew nothing about modern ideas, so stuck-in-the-box they were. Hell, one time I was touring one of our buildings and I saw one of the workmen arguing with an architect over what panes of glass we should use, and the workman's idea was infinitely better—it made the rooms feel more open with lots more natural light. I almost fired the architect because of it!"

"Yes," I replied, "and that's the reason I went in business, to try to give new ideas to architects and designers, and build them. For example, one day on a project, I came into the building, and it was so dark I could hardly see anything in front of my face. The previous night I had read up on large-scale double-paned glass with an added fiber mesh that, so that giant skylights wouldn't break. When I told the architect about the lighting issue and how to fix it, the guy started yelling at me, saying that I was just a carpenter, and I didn't have the degree he had."

"Hah!" the gentleman burst out and laughed. "*You* were that guy! I knew I recognized you!"

"You worked on the Vernon Welsh Library?"

"You could say that."

"I'm terrible with faces. May I have your name?"

"Vernon. Vernon Welsh."

My jaw dropped. This man was one of the top business leaders in New England. He owned furniture stores, car dealerships, a small fast-food franchise, and a bunch of other assorted companies. He had commissioned the Vernon Welsh Public Library I had worked on a few years back. I heard he paid for nearly the entire thing himself.

I stuttered, "Mr. Welsh . . . ah . . . It's a pleasure."

"Please call me Vern. You know, I was certainly impressed by your work, so I assume your business must be doing well."

With nothing to lose and no one else to talk to, I aired my complaints. "I have got a good job that I'm working on, but I end up working more and more hours a day. I can't spend any time with my wife; I don't have any 'me' time, and, after all my expenses, I'm making less than I did when I worked for someone else. I thought I was fulfilling my dream to be a builder-architect, but now I could care less! I just want to take control of my life!"

Vern sank into his chair and sighed. Part of me hoped he'd just tell me to go back to my old job and close the business. He sighed again and sat back up and looked me dead in the eye. "So, you want to take control of your life?"

"Yes!"

"Good! At least, that's a start. Some just want to give up the first time they fail. Not many learn from their mistakes, to actually shape their own destinies." He paused and pulled out a small notepad from his coat pocket and scribbled down a few things. He tore out the page of paper and handed it to me, pointing at the first line. His handwriting was hard to read, but I could make out the word "Plan."

"What's your plan?" he asked.

I thought for a minute. "What plan?" I said coyly. "Can the plan be there is no plan?"

He didn't seem very surprised and gave only a slight sigh. "No plan?" he said. "That is why most businesses fail. Answer this—where would you like to be in the next three years?"

I hadn't looked at my situation that way. I knew what I wanted and what I was hoping for. Did that count? "I would like to be able to do what I love and not have to work so much that I start hating it. I also want to be able to take personal time. Money is a factor too, but if I had just a bit of freedom, I would be happy."

"A noble goal—though a tad vague. Now, how will you accomplish it?"

"I have no idea."

*Did this man have patience, or what?*

"All right," he said as he pointed to the next scribbled note: "Goal Setting." "So you know your *general* goal. Here is how you make it into a *specific* goal." He handed me another sheet. I read through the sub-points: measurable, accountable, defined time frame, written. He continued, "Make your goals measurable and translate your big-picture objectives into something quantifiable. In your case, in three years' time, for example, 'I want to take my sixty hour weeks and turn them into thirty hour weeks with X-amount of vacation days a year.'"

I nodded as he moved along. "Accountability means knowing who is held responsible for every aspect of the goal," he said. "Right now, that is just you. Down the road, employees and managers might be responsible for fulfilling parts of the goal, but right now it is all on you."

I gulped. "Responsibility" always felt like a heavy word to me.

"Define your time frame," he continued, "not just three years, but what happens in between to achieve that goal. Define certain objectives every week to keep yourself on track. And, finally, write it down. Expand on any goal. Keep it written down. If someone else is responsible for an aspect of that goal, get a signature so they can be held accountable." He handed me the notepad and pen. "Well, go on."

I felt like I was back in grade school. I started writing. "In three years' time, I want to make twice as much as I did when I was employed, work only thirty hours a week, and have three weeks out of the year to spend time with my family."

As I was writing this down, Vern summarized, "Goal-setting is the process that drives your business forward. Whether it is company-wide, 'big-picture' goals or narrow, specific goals for a particular employee, setting goals is one of the most important duties of a leader." He jerked the pad out of my hand, my pen trailed a line off the page as he did.

He looked at what I had written. "Good. Not great, but, at least, it is written now."

He continued his impromptu class. "Right now you are self-employed—you are not running a business. A one-person business works in some cases, like for psychiatrists, lawyers, and a few professions, but their success is completely tied to their actions; if they get sick, they don't make money." He paused. "Think about it like this: Do you need to hammer every nail when you work? It takes hours of your time, and the task isn't that specialized, so why not outsource it or hire someone else to do it? Your time needs to be focused on the highly skilled aspects of your business. Delegating some or part of your jobs not only frees up time but also allows you to expand. Instead of working on just one project, you could work on two, or three, or a hundred!"

Everything he said made sense. I knew he was right.

"In the beginning," he continued, "when you get your first employee, not only you will have to be the owner but also a manager. At some point, you might get a manager—and be careful who you hire in that role—but for now, if you can manage and delegate tasks, you will do more and have more time and be able to make the most of it. We'll talk more on this later." He lowered his head to scratch more on the tiny notepad.

I sipped at my coffee. Vern must have seen my reaction to its coldness and waved to me to get another for both of us. When I returned with our coffee, Vern pushed a few sheets of paper in front of me and started talking again. "You should start understanding the *purpose* behind your actions." Then, pointing to the first sheet, he said, "If you focus only on the short-term future, it is easy to lose your sense of motivation. Sound familiar?"

Yes, too familiar. I took a sip of my latte.

"The drudgery of daily work piles up," he said, "and the only prize awaiting you upon completion is another stack of work the next day.

To stay motivated and productive, you have to remember your core purpose—your long-term goal. What is it? That is the question you must answer because as soon as you take your eyes off the prize and instead focus on the short-term battles, you'll get discouraged and apathetic. My guess is that is where you are. Right?" He looked straight at me. I nodded; he had hit the bull's eye.

He continued, "Now you're probably asking yourself how to stay enthusiastic when you feel like a failure. Instead, ask yourself why you started your business in the first place. I have found over the years that the key to dealing with failure is not so much how you respond to it when it happens; rather, the key is keeping failure in proper perspective by how you approach it to begin with. Look, while failure is *inevitable,* failure is never *final.* Just think, Abraham Lincoln ran for a federal political office six times. Four times he lost. He only won two of those elections—once for the U.S. House of Representatives and once for the presidency. You *are* going to fail, in both big ways and small ways. Business acquisitions or expansions *will* backfire. Employees *will* quit. Rather than viewing each of these events as a setback, acknowledge them as progress toward your ultimate success. In my view, every failure presents the opportunity to learn, and each one moves you that much closer to success. They're stepping stones on the road to your goal. As a business owner, you cannot afford to succumb to negativity. You set the tone for your business." Keeping his eye on me, Vern picked up his coffee and started sipping.

"It can't be that simple," I said. "I can't just turn around my company overnight! I can't just become the next, well, *you,* just by doing these things!" I thought for a moment before blurting, "What makes great companies great?"

"You're right," he replied, "it does take time, but you just raised one of the most important questions, and if there were an easy answer, we would all be billionaires." He paused. "What makes great companies great, you ask?" He began jotting on the notepad again while talking, "What do world-class businesses do that everybody else doesn't?" He pushed a sheet of paper over to me. "I consider these four traits fundamental to every highly successful business. I have applied them to my own businesses. Here they are:

"First, *commitment to creating value*. Great businesses understand the mindset of their customers. When introducing new products and services, the focus is first and foremost adding value for the customer. The iPhone is a perfect example of this concept. Apple understood that consumers weren't going to buy their phones because of an impressive list of features; they were going to buy the phone that made their life better and easier. That is why the marketing campaign for the iPhone never focused on the product's specs. It focused on how the product would make life better or easier."

Right, I thought. Dave Cowen wasn't interested in the specs of the windows and swivels and drop-away theater; what he heard was that he'd get two rooms in one. With a push of a button, life would be better for him.

Vern slid another piece under my nose.

"Second, every business needs *a sense of purpose*. Successful businesses are about more than making money. I mean, that's not why you went in business, correct? At the end of the day, you must be driven by something beyond money, or passion burns out. What is your purpose? What are you passionate about? Jeff Bezos, at Amazon, was committed to reinventing the shopping experience. Think about it—not too long ago it took weeks to deliver a package. Now you press a button and within twenty-four hours it's at your door! Successful businesses always have underlying goals that are about more than making money."

Things were starting to click. I didn't just want to make money; I wanted to make buildings that would last, stand the test of time, and not just because no one wanted to tear them down, but because those buildings would be revolutionary!

Vern must have seen a glint of excitement in my eyes. He smiled as he handed me another sheet of paper. It said in all caps: "STRONG, VISIONARY LEADERSHIP." Then, with new vigor in his voice, he continued.

"Third is *innovation*. In my experience, there are two types of businesses: those that innovate and those that follow. Innovation doesn't have to be dramatic. You don't have to come up with the next great revolutionary business model, but you do have to find a way to do something better than your competition and in a way that is meaningful to your customer. This can mean providing better customer service, or developing a game-changing product or service, or running a brilliant marketing campaign. Innovation allows you to set yourself above the competition because they're not doing what you are doing. To be innovative, a company must have strong, forward-thinking leadership. These leaders must be able to spot an opportunity, develop a plan to take advantage of it. They then effectively communicate that plan to their employees. You must keep your vigor, and lead the direction of the company!"

His passion was rubbing off on me, and I felt more hopeful than I had in a long time. "But how do that passion and vision help me *now?*" I asked. "I have bills to pay!"

He looked perplexed for a second. "Everything revolves around the long term. If you set up your steps for the long term, the short term will come naturally."

"But what about *now?*" I insisted.

Vern paused and sighed and launched into another monologue. "Never get stuck in the short term . . ."

I felt like a child in front of a teacher. I was angry for no reason. All his advice seemed right on the money, but it didn't seem to matter in the present. I wanted to cut him off again but decided to let him go on, and listen as he continued.

"Short-term thinking, and sometimes acting impulsively, can be a strength, but if you get stuck in the here and now, you'll inevitably make mistakes that can cost you the future. Look at what happened to you. When you started your business, did you attempt to foresee where you would go? Or did you just think about tomorrow and the freedom you thought your business would give to you? Now your business is sinking, and you are panicking, afraid, worried. Maybe you are also feeling trapped?"

"OK, OK," I said. "I keep getting stuck in short-term thinking, but what can I do?"

Vern sighed again. "I know where you're coming from. As a business owner, you spend time planning, most likely on the short-term *operational* planning, creating your production schedule, and so forth, but you have to learn to spend at the very least a couple of hours a month engaged in *strategic* planning. Your analysis of your current market was right, but don't forget to make projections for the future. For example, the materials or technology you use today might not be the same you'll use down the line. Take stock of your market from time to time. Who are your competitors? Have they changed their business model, marketing strategy, or other tactics recently?

"Along with this, keep an eye for innovation. The key to creating your status as a leader in your market is to stay ahead of the curve. You can do this to a degree by paying attention to your customers, listening to their feedback, frustrations, desires, and so forth. As the business owner, it is your job to look for opportunities to innovate—whether they're obvious to your customers or not."

At least, this kind of thinking was familiar to me. It made me also think that on my next project, I should talk more with the customer, to see what more or new or different things I could do.

Vern then said, "The fourth thing you should focus on is *sustainability*. As you, and even I, have demonstrated, we act impulsively from time to time. Our bias towards action can be a source of strength. That being said, remember not to overextend yourself as you seek to innovate. Instead, create systems for your business operations so that they are sustainable and repeatable. To be a world-class business, it is important for you to spend time planning for the long term, while also regularly planning for the short term."

Even as he let out a deep breath as if exhausted, I could tell this was a topic he loved to speak about. Questions poured into my head. *Could it truly be done?* There was one question in particular that I had on my mind. "But Vern, what you say seems like it applies to your specialty, big business. I don't get how it applies to small ones like mine."

I saw a look of exasperation come across his face. *Was I that thick-headed?*

"Humph," he grunted. "When I first started in the business world, I took over my father's photography business. It was a simple mom-and-pop shop that he had started when my brothers and I were just kids. For years, I watched my father scrape by in the same way you are. He started out loving photography—every element from taking pictures to developing them to selling them. I remember some days coming down to his lab and watching him use a single-hair brush to touch up his photos. It was a job that took him hours at a time." He paused. "By the time my brothers and I were ready for college, his passion of so many years was all but gone. I started helping out at the shop by doing a few small tasks. One day I came across his account books. He was deeply in the red. That day I made a choice: I knew there wasn't enough money for my brothers and me to all go to college, so I chose to stay and work. Didn't take much convincing my father to let me take over many elements of the shop. He spent the next few years taking photographs while I did everything else. After the first few months of working at the shop, I decided we needed to expand. I believed we could become more, grow a bigger business, and serve more people. With the money I had saved from various high school jobs I hired a second photographer, and purchased a second camera and other equipment for him to use. When he wasn't photographing, he helped with a few miscellaneous tasks. During that period, I wrote down my goals. At first, they were very broad, and soon I realized I couldn't do much with them, so I made them specific. I asked myself how I could accomplish each goal. Being young and having a lot of energy was an advantage, I guess. Even when I hit roadblocks, I just sat down and wrote out how to overcome them.

"Within a few years, I managed to grow the company to a five-studio operation spread across New England, with twenty photographers and marketers, managers, and salespeople. The mom-and-pop shop was gone; we had nearly a hundred employees and were grossing a few million a year. After that, I took the leap and started investing in other industries. The rest is history."

He took another sip of coffee, seeming disappointed that it was almost empty. "Nothing I've told you is going to make your business successful. Success is up to you. You'll have to implement these ideas for yourself and overcome all the hurdles."

I wished I could wrap Vern up in a box and take him home. "But what if I hit a stumbling block?" I asked. "I can't imagine business has a crystal ball for solutions. Could I possibly ask you?"

"Hah! I'm not a business consultant, Jack. But I feel I owe you one for the library project. Here's my card. Now, I certainly won't drop everything and come running whenever you call, but if you need help I'm sure you can keep buying me some coffee!"

Beaming, I reached for the business card, "Thank you, Vern. Earlier today I felt trapped, and I do have some things to work out, but maybe I can get through this."

"Well that's good," he said as he stood up. "Just remember, you must implement anything and everything you learn. Your business reflects you, your vigor, your vision, and your passion. Even when you think times are darkest, there's always a way to get through; just look for it." As he headed for the door, he looked back and said, "Good luck, Jack."

It was late. The rain had turned into a light fog, but even in the dark, I could see the mist lifting. Walking to my car, I couldn't help but smile; while taking the first steps in my business had seemed so simple, now I had a much clearer vision of the long road forward.

"I will succeed," I whispered to myself. "I've just got a lot of work to do." I had never realized how over the years fear had dragged me down. How I was feeling about my business was just one example of these mental blocks. For the first time, though, my fear didn't seem to matter. Everything Vern said was sinking in. I felt the wheels in my mind turning, thoughts clicking, and lights turning on everywhere, like fireworks.

I was still smiling as I pulled into the driveway. Before going upstairs, I went to my study and found some paper. I jotted myself a note: "In three years' time I want to be making twice as much as when I was employed, work only thirty hours a week, and have three weeks out of the year to spend time with my family."

I heard Erica call from the bedroom, "Hey, honey, it's past ten. How about coming up to bed?"

*OK, I'll finish this in the morning.*

# Chapter 4
## METAMORPHOSIS

A t five o'clock the alarm rang its morning wake-up call. I heard Erica stirring. After a moment, I bumbled down the stairs in exhaustion. The words Vern had spoken seemed to loom over me.

My plan for the morning was simple: get breakfast and write up my goals. I had three hours before I had to be on the job.

After grabbing my coffee, I sat down at the kitchen counter. I had already written one overarching goal at the top of the page, with a bunch of dots below it. I felt like a painter staring at an empty canvas.

"Three years," I said to myself. "That's my goal. I can't plan out my life in the course of a few hours, but I can create a structure to work with." I remembered Vern's advice: long-term thinking doesn't help the short term. I'll have to fit the short term into the long term, but I'll address the long term later. Would I regret this approach? Perhaps. But I had to finish at least this much this morning.

I started my list.

Week one: Hire my first employee, explore the market and expand my enterprise. Oh boy, I thought, I was already going way over my head. What could I accomplish in the next week, the next month? How would these add up to my longer term vision and goals?

I continued writing. Within the next two weeks, I'll make Jack's Modern Design profitable, successful, and capable of growth.

How the heck would I accomplish this? I paused. Why was I failing? For one, I was overstretched and working all the time, but only on one project at any given time. I was doing all the work myself, but there were tons of tasks I could give to an employee. But could I manage someone? I realized that when I worked for GBH, I often had to help out the less experienced carpenters working with me. I must be able to manage! By hiring a carpenter for less than I was making, I could at the very least create more time for myself. It seemed like win-win, and I could use that time for expanding my business.

I looked down at the paper. Suddenly things seemed less overwhelming. Planning a few weeks ahead was easy: write it down and spend a couple of hours a week planning. Perhaps the long run would work itself out as I went along!

I needed to include a brief team meeting at the start of the work day, a huddle to keep all connected and focused on the tasks for the day.

I now had my goals for the coming weeks: hire a new carpenter (under that, put out an online advertisement), and study up on the interviewing and hiring process. Maybe send Vern an email?

I heard a noise from upstairs. It sounded like Erica was just getting up. Wow, I must have spent an hour already just getting to this point. I looked at the paper. What else could I do in the next few weeks to help accomplish my three-year goal?

Find new customers.

How could I accomplish this? I didn't know how to market. Put out online feelers? But would that get customers interested in my specific services? But I was already hemorrhaging cash, so any new work would help.

Having begun by writing down a few steps, I felt calmer. I continued writing: Put together marketing materials, put out marketing online, set aside time to work with customers. I moved through the list in this fashion. It wasn't pretty, and it was very short term. I jotted down a few more personal notes and technical things I needed for my current work. I felt on track. I sent Vern a quick email to ask about what I should look for in hiring my first employee.

Going to the job that day wasn't so bad. But while I felt inspired about my plans, I started viewing my daily work as, well, tedious. Every time I picked up a power tool I thought that someone else could be doing this and that I could be working on the larger picture. Soon.

My phone beeped at me. A new email. I scrolled through the messages. Vern had responded with a substantial message. This is what it said:

*Dear Jack,*

*For a small business owner, making that first hire is among the most important decisions you will ever make. The right employee will become your invaluable right hand, allowing you to grow your business. On the other hand, a poor hire will undermine your efforts to build your business. And while there is no way to guarantee a successful hire, here are a few ideas that I have used over the years to maximize my chances of making a great hire:*

- *Take your time. With a decision this crucial, you would think this goes without saying. Unfortunately, by the time most business owners realize they need help, they are so overwhelmed that they are willing to hire the first person* who applies. No matter how busy you are, it is worth taking the time to thoroughly evaluate your options to make the best hire.

- *Look for a good personal fit. While you should not expect every employee you hire to become a friend, it is important that you get along well with each one, especially the first one. The two of you will be working closely together, and if either of you rub the other the wrong way; it is going to be a difficult environment for both of you. Spend substantial time in conversation during the interview process and try to get a feel for personality as well as ability.*

- *Look for complementary skills. Until you hire your first employee, you are handling every aspect of your operation. The purpose of hiring an employee will be to assign some of your responsibility to him or her—so make sure that their strengths complement yours. Often we are most drawn to individuals with similar skills and passions as our own. Look for a complement, not a clone!*

- *Seek out plenty of applicants. Conduct several rounds of interviews. And carry out your due diligence. A good rule of thumb is to think "3x3," interview at least three people and interview those three people at least three times.*

*Sorry, I didn't have time to include more. There are many resources you can look into; just remember to take your time. I understand you feel rushed but hiring the wrong person this early can cause irreversible damage to your business.*

*Wishing you the best,*
*Vern*

I took note of the second point—a good fit. I may not have been the greatest people person in the world, but I usually understood the people with whom I clicked. Moving down the list, I already knew what I needed—someone to do the unspecialized work, that shouldn't be an issue.

The housing project I was on was almost finished. I decided that when I got home, I would post on a looking-to-hire website for an unskilled carpenter. While I was at it, so I wouldn't get left high and dry, I would also post on a classified advertisement website for more work.

That night I began drafting my looking-to-hire advertisement. Advertising for jobs seemed the easiest to do first because it revolved almost entirely around my work experience:

---

Call Jack's Modern Design at 1-555-555-5243!

Why hire a big no-name construction company and pay all their overhead?

Call us! Hire the guys who will actually do work and save you money!

As a licensed carpenter with over a decade of experience, Jack's Modern Design do more than simply build your project, we will help improve it as well! We use all the latest techniques in modern design to make your project look remarkable—and last for years!

We will always answer your call!

---

I was glad that was done. I hoped someone responded quickly. Now I needed to write up the hiring document and send it off. It seemed fairly easy and didn't need to be too specific—I just needed an unskilled laborer who can do the tasks that drained my time and energy.

---

Jack's Modern Design

Looking for an unskilled carpenter, minimal experience is fine, I can teach you on the job.

Job Description: You will work on general carpentry work, laying cement/concrete, putting up dry-wall, etc.; you will create and maintain a safe work site environment; Communicate with management.

Requirements and Qualifications: Current Driver's License with clean driving record

Compensation: Based on experience

Email: jmdJack118@gmail.com

Phone: 1-555-555-5243

---

That seemed like a good start. It wasn't as specific as it should have been, but I just needed some help and some new jobs. Someday I would have my own website. Someday I would hire someone to do the marketing for both customers and new employees.

"Someday," I said under my breath. I heard the start of rain on the windows and looked out. An ominous fog seemed to surround the house. Good thing I didn't believe in portents. Today I had taken the first step in making my business an actual business, and I wasn't going to let a bit of bad weather get me down.

Over the course of the next few days, I clutched my phone continuously, anxious for responses to my ads. But no one called: no hires, no jobs. I couldn't help but wonder if I had listed the wrong phone number. Wasn't there anyone out there interested in working with me? Wasn't there anyone looking for my services? After a few days I became despondent—but then I felt a vibration in my pocket. I looked at my phone. It was a 508 number—from somewhere in the central and southern part of the state—and a number I didn't recognize. Yes! Finally! Was it my next future employee? A new customer? I held my breath.

With my luck, it would just be a telemarketer.

I answered, "Jack's Modern Design, this is Jack, how can I help you?"

"Hello, this is John Goodall. I saw your advertisement online. I have an unfinished basement that I'd like turned into an office space." I listened to John speak as he went into detail. The space was roughly 1,500 square feet and had to be configured to include a work area, meeting area and kitchenette. But most importantly, he offered $100,000 for labor if the job would be done in the next two months.

"I'll need to take a look at the basement itself to see what I'm dealing with," I told him, "and draw up the materials and the costs. Once I do that, I can give you an estimate for the full job." Even I could hear the excitement in my voice. We set up a time next week to meet.

It was a perfect opportunity. It meant that once the housing project was done, I would be able to move on—and for good money too!

There was a problem, though. To meet John's time frame, I would need additional help. But fate was on my side because, over the course of the next few days, I received five emails from various people who saw my hiring ad. Four of them were young and very inexperienced—I think only one of them had ever in his life held a hammer—while the fifth was a licensed carpenter with five years' experience. It seemed like a good pool of applicants to start with. Even though I already thought I knew which one to hire, I set up interviews with them all.

Interview day came. The countdown clock to the basement project was ticking away. I started with the first three. As I expected, they hadn't a clue about carpentry. Each was a college student looking for work to help pay his way through school. I understood where they were coming from, and part of me wanted to hire them all; but if I did, I would spend way too much time instructing them on the most basic things. I didn't have the time to do that, and I couldn't risk having them make mistakes.

The fourth of the group, a young man in his early twenties named Everett, sat down with me at the coffee shop where I was conducting the interviews. From his résumé it seemed he had only held a few odd jobs, and only one of them was construction related. At least, he had some experience, I thought.

Everett had an air of energy that was contagious, and I couldn't help but smile. "So Everett, it doesn't look like you have much experience in construction, which is fine, but I obviously can't hire someone who doesn't know how to hold a hammer."

"Work-wise, that's right," he chuckled. "I haven't had many jobs as a carpenter, but when I was young, I frequently helped my father with projects around the house. I loved to build things. I built my first birdhouse when I was just five. I wanted to go to college to become an engineer, but money was a problem. I have taken a bunch of community college classes over the past few years and worked a few jobs to help pay for my living. At this point, I think college is out of my reach, so I want to get into carpentry. I was good at it when I was a kid, and I figured I could get some valuable experience working for you so I could get on with becoming a licensed carpenter."

I had Everett tell me some more about projects he'd done. From what he described, he was right—he did have the basic skills.

I made my decision. "You've got the job," I told Everett. "There are a few things we'll review on site, but if you are ready and willing, you can start next week." We shook hands, and he left. As far as I was concerned, I just hired the perfect first employee.

I had one more interview to go. The man was about my age who had a solid portfolio and five years' experience as a licensed carpenter. He was due at the coffee shop in five minutes. I grabbed a cappuccino. I didn't know why I was bothering with this interview; after all, we already had a master carpenter—me—and I had just hired an additional hand.

A short, dazed-looking, beer-bellied man walked in. He looked over the tables as if searching for something. *This must be the guy.* I waved him over to my table. He lit up as he walked over and sat down.

"Name's Tom," he said, "but you can call me Tommy if you like."

"You know, Tommy, I'm not looking for a licensed contractor. I just need someone to do some menial labor."

He held up both his hands. "Hey, that's fine. I just need some part-time work for now. My wife just had some surgery and needs help at home. She can't work for now, so I'm shouldering the workload for my family. I'm willing to take almost any job that pays and can give me the time I need."

I felt terrible for Tommy. I remembered when I had to drop out of college to help care for my family, and I understood what he was going through. I didn't need a skilled carpenter—it would cost me too much. But I didn't want to leave this man out on the street either. I asked him for more details of his work history. He certainly seemed good at what he did, a by-the-books builder. I didn't need him, but I felt for him. Wasn't that a good enough reason to hire him? Besides, then I would have someone who could instruct Everett if I couldn't be around.

"All right, you've got the job," I said as I extended my hand. I told him about the basement project and that he'd be starting next week.

"Oh, thank you, thank you," he replied. "I was worried I wouldn't find a new job before my rent was due. You are a real life saver."

I gave myself a mental pat on the back.

I slept easy that night: not only had my business gained two new employees but I had also done a good deed. The housing project was coming to a close, and the basement project was about to start and tomorrow. My three-year goal suddenly felt much closer.

I woke up bright-eyed and bushy-tailed. Meeting my second client felt like a bigger and more exhilarating step than the first. My business was up and running.

The drive to the home took me nearly an hour, passing from suburbs, through neighborhoods, past farmlands, and into the boonies. The house turned out to be a mansion on a private street, in a small cul-de-sac, overlooking a picturesque pond. Everything about it was massive, including nine-foot entry doors and a thirty-foot entryway.

The owner, John Goodall approached. "Hey Jack, good to see you. Let me show you what we need you to do." He took me to the basement. It had massive ceilings, too. It was completely unfinished, and the cement floor was moist—this would present a few issues. There was a boiler, a furnace, and an oil tank in the far corner that would require an additional wall to cover up. There certainly were a few challenges to overcome.

I spoke with John about what needed to be done. He wasn't looking for anything fancy, certainly nothing requiring my level of expertise, but a job's a job, I thought to myself. I gave him a rough estimate of material costs. With two new employees, this job would be easy. We agreed on a price and a timeframe.

At the beginning of the job we all worked together. I had Tommy watch over Everett and instruct him. Then I got a call on another job—small housing project that needed a new kitchen for one of the houses. The client was looking for some unique designs for aesthetically building the kitchen appliances into a stone framing. Right up my alley. I figured I could go there the next day, and everything at the Goodall house would proceed on schedule with Tommy overseeing the work. I talked with him about it. "Jack, don't worry. I got this," he assured me.

*Great! I've got people I can trust to do some of my jobs.* This was the first step toward the future. Someday I would be able to leave my work for days at a time and know that things would still get done.

Erica was preparing dinner when I got home. I ran up and hugged her. "Jack, what's gotten into you?" she laughed.

"My business is going to work, hon. I can finally earn a decent living and someday we'll be able to take some good alone time."

"Whoa there, cowboy, don't get ahead of yourself. This is the first time you have left Tommy and Everett alone to manage themselves. I mean, this is bound to happen, but we can't afford to be this hopeful. What if things go wrong?"

Negative Nancy, I thought to myself. She didn't even know Tommy or Everett; how could she judge them?

The next day I went to the kitchen job. I was intrigued by what the designer had to say. And although she didn't fully understand the various avenues we could take for aesthetically integrating the appliances into the design, it was just the kind of work I always wanted to do. It wasn't so much architecture, yet the art of it seemed to flow out of me, and I got the job. I would have some time, even in the midst of the Goodall basement project, so we settled on beginning work next week. Everett would continue to learn on the job.

I couldn't have been more proud of myself: two deals and two new employees in the course of a week. I darted back to the basement project, listening to the happiest music I could find on the radio. *What could go wrong?*

Half skipping into the basement, I looked down: the hardwood was installed! *What?* There was no way the sealing could have settled in already; the stuff takes over a week to properly set. I saw Everett slogging away at the last few panels. "Everett! Why the heck are you installing the hardwood?"

"Tommy told me to start laying it down. Mr. Goodall gave him the 'what-for' when he saw the instructions on the sealant packets. He said it would cost valuable time! I swear! I just did what Tommy said. It seemed right at the time. After all, it's what the customer wanted." Everett seemed panicked.

I took a deep, long breath, "Do you realize that without first sealing the concrete floor, the wood is going to absorb humidity like a sponge in a steam bath? This floor won't last the fifteen years I guaranteed. In fact, we'll be lucky if it lasts five without cracking!"

"Don't tell *me* that!" Everett protested. "I know the issue, but Tommy thought that the customer was right, even though *he* knew it was wrong. But he thought he had to do everything the customer said."

I almost screamed. The customer wasn't always right. Just because they wanted a thing done a certain way didn't mean, that was the right way to do it! Nobody wins that way!

"Tommy!" I yelled at the top of my lungs.

He ran in. "What?"

"Do you realize what you've done?" My voice seethed with anger.

Tommy looked at me incredulously. "Jack, I just did what the customer ordered. You weren't here, so what was I supposed to do? He said to do the floor today, or we'll get behind schedule. Who cares if he was right or wrong? It didn't matter to me, so I went ahead and did it!"

I paused. Maybe I couldn't fault him. But it wasn't what I would ever do or what this company should ever do. Tommy should have known that, so why did he just go with what the customer said? Why didn't he call me? Goodall cared about a lasting product. It should have been easy enough to explain the situation to him.

"Tommy," I said in a controlled, emotionless voice, "we need to focus on making an enduring product, the best quality product possible. I wanted to give John the office space of a lifetime. How can it be for a lifetime if we are just focused on deadlines? We could have still made the deadline with the sealant; how hard would it have been to explain that?"

With a look of honest regret, he responded, "Jack, I'm sorry, but when you hired me I assumed it was to get jobs done. How was I supposed to know we would have to confront the customer sometimes? I had always been told that the customer is always right!"

I sighed. Everyone always hears that platitude, but it isn't always true. Sometimes the customer expects the job to be done a certain way but doesn't understand what it takes to get the outcome they want. "Tommy," I said, "I think I may have misrepresented this company to you. We stand for innovation, for quality, and for products that will last through the ages. This will mean, that occasionally, we have to tell the customer about *our* way of doing things. Sure the customer is always right, but we can still help them understand . . ." I trailed off and went silent.

It seemed as though the ground had shook beneath my feet and the skies had opened to release a heavenly rain. I had just described my company's purpose—a purpose I had never expressed.

Suddenly, I knew what to say.

"Tommy, tear up the flooring. Try to save as much of the hardwood as you can. Everett, help him out. We are going to put the sealant down. I'll talk to Mr. Goodall." I realized that this might cost us a couple grand to straighten out, but what I just learned was worth more than that. My company, my employees, and I now had a clear purpose, a set of beliefs, and a set of values. I knew it wouldn't be an overnight project to spell everything out, but I had the beginning formulation of the company's motto: We stand for innovation, for quality, and for products that will last through the ages."

One of the business books that I had read said that proper delegation requires setting clear expectations, being sure the employee has the ability to take on the challenge and, then as a manager, follow up in a timely manner. I also remember that the opposite of delegation is *abdication*—simply tossing the proverbial "hot potato" and hoping the employee will do the job right.

# Chapter 5
## ANGER AND ACCEPTANCE

A few months had past, and Jack's Modern Design seemed to be growing by itself. More jobs had been rolling in such that I needed more hands, not only with the jobs themselves but also with accounting, billing and a bunch of other paperwork details. It seemed like I would soon need an office.

My first administrative employee was a young woman named Lisa. She had a genius-like finesse with numbers and could do the books in a quarter of the time it took me. And when she wasn't balancing each week's figures, she organized my emails, took calls, updated my old advertisements, and even started hunting for a website designer. It seemed like I hardly had to manager her.

With Lisa's improvements to our marketing, customers found us more easily. I still wasn't overly picky about the jobs I would take because, right now, a monthly cash balance was a higher priority; but gradually, the jobs people wanted done were more like what we wanted to do.

One day we received a request to bid on a full-blown hotel refurbishing where the clients wanted a new and creative design to make the building "pop." It would be a big job with a big payoff—my biggest job to date.

The dilapidated Colonial Hotel had twenty guest rooms, a lobby, a kitchen, and a dining room. All of it needed renovation. And the exterior . . . don't even get me started on that. I was amazed someone hadn't already been injured by falling debris from the deteriorating bricks. Some multinational conglomerate had bought the place. For whatever reason, they loved the location of this dusty, dying building. I agonized over a proposal to make the building stand out both visually and technologically, yet was amazed when my plan was selected.

I had two new hires for this job: David and Daniel Funar, two freshly licensed carpenters, originally from Romania. They were brothers—in fact, they were twins. But each had a different work style: Daniel always seemed to want to work quickly—not to the point of being reckless, but at times he would miss small details in his haste. He was also prone to making snap judgments. David, on the other hand, was painstakingly meticulous in his efforts, often to the point of getting too wrapped in the smallest projects. Ironically, I only noticed this when they were working on separate projects because, when they worked together, their differences seemed to cancel out and they were very productive.

Ever since the Goodall basement job a few months back, to keep an eye on things, I felt like I had to be on site, working side-by-side with my staff. I had paid a few grand out of pocket to fix that flooring mistake. This meant I had to work extra hours. Following the end of the regular workday, I had to set up plans, meet clients, and provide proposals. I was, at least, still a step ahead of where I was when I first started. While I still wasn't making as much personal money as when I had a job working for someone else, at least, my business was holding its own.

On a sunny afternoon, I was at the Colonial Hotel site going over some drawings. Suddenly I heard a loud *crash*.

*What the . . .?*

I ran into the next room to see what happened. The twins were shouting at each other in Romanian and looking at the ceiling above the wall they had been gutting. Pieces of the floor above were hanging down through the ceiling.

"Hey! What's going on here?" I asked. "What the heck happened?"

They're yelling at each other irritated me more than parts of the ceiling and wall having collapsed.

In his thick Eastern European accent, David said, "Jack, when we got through the dry-wall we came across some sort of chicken wire on both sides of the wall running up the length of the building. Daniel yanked on it, and the ceiling gave way. Maybe there used to be a door here. The previous owners did a lousy job. If you want, Daniel and I can take out all this wire from this whole section by the end of the day and tomorrow we can patch it all up."

Looking at the mess, I sighed, "No, just be ready to patch up this wall and the upstairs wall. We can't take the time or spend the resources on the entire wall."

"But this is a hazard!" David said. "It's amazing these walls lasted as long as they did! I thought you cared about quality. These walls are anything but quality! Let us do what you pay us to do!"

I stared at the mess on the floor. David was right. I couldn't sacrifice quality. But after what he and Daniel just did, how could I trust them not to accidently tear down the entire building? Sure they were good carpenters, but they weren't me.

"You're right, David," I said. "I'll take care of the walls while you guys finish the flooring with Everett. Tommy has to leave soon so I'm sure Everett could use a hand."

Shaking his head, he was dumbstruck.

First Daniel quickly said, "With only one person working on them, these walls could take a few days!"

"Everett can do the floors by himself," added David. "He has learned plenty over the past few months, and flooring isn't hard!"

"If you work alone you might get injured!" said Daniel.

The two of them continued for a couple of minutes, talking so fast I thought they were switching in and out of Romanian at times.

Finally, I held up my hand. "Don't worry, I got this. Just go help Everett."

"*Neisprăvit*," Daniel mumbled. I had no idea what that meant, but the tone was unmistakably an insult. Was he calling me an idiot? Everett looked up from his work, and Tommy, who was just heading off, glanced over as if he were waiting to see what I would do. The tension in the air was unnerving. I grimaced at Daniel but chose not to call him out on it. They were right after all; this job would be easier with two working on it.

This was the first time I had butted heads with the twins, but it wasn't the first conflict that had happened since the basement project. Some days Everett insisted he could do his jobs himself, but I wasn't about to let him work alone. Tommy seemed to understand my frustrations, but he still seemed to feel bad for costing me money on that project. He even kept a copy of "company beliefs" in his shirt pocket. Everett seemed on board with the company's beliefs, but he also wanted more freedom on the job. He'd frequently say, "Just tell me what you want to be done. I'll ask if I need help." I would always tell him, though, that I needed someone with experience to check up on him. And although it always seemed to make a difference to have Tommy working with Everett, frequently Tommy would leave Everett to do his own thing.

The hours ticked by as I labored intensely to pull the damnable chicken wire out of the wall. *Who pours concrete over chicken wire?* I was well behind schedule, and there was no way was going to finish gutting it by the end of the day. I waived to Everett and the twins as they were leaving. Daniel still looked angered and didn't wave back. David waved before patting his brother on the back as they left. He then turned his head toward me and mouthed, "Good luck."

I was there for another four hours.

Getting out of the car that night, the evaporation from my sweat-soaked t-shirt made me feel like I was freezing. I didn't even eat dinner. I mustered up just enough energy to send Vern an email from my phone asking him if he would have lunch tomorrow before taking a quick shower and crawling into bed. I fell dead asleep the moment my head touched the pillow. I didn't even hear my phone buzz with Vern's reply, "Sure, same old coffee shop?"

The next morning at the Colonial Hotel, the vibe felt odd. While Daniel was polite, he still seemed irked. He, David, and Everett had ripped up nearly all the old flooring and were laying down the sealant to deal with the mold. I worked away at the giant hole I had made in the wall. I could see straight up through the wall structure for four stories. It was going to be another long day. At least, I would have a break when I met Vern for lunch.

By noon, I had done only the first floor. It was slow going, and I was covered in concrete and plaster. I dusted myself off and headed out to meet up with Vern.

Walking into the coffee shop, I noticed the waitress staring at me. I glanced at my reflection in the window: my hair was covered with bits of plaster. I ordered my coffee before sitting down. It felt like yesterday that I was at this same table where I had first met Vern when I felt on the verge of closing up shop. Now, months later, even though business was booming, something still didn't feel right.

Vern walked in and hung up his woolen overcoat and fedora on the coat rack. His glance around the room seemed to pass right over my head. Suddenly, his gaze rebounded and caught my eye. He strolled over.

"Jack, you look terrible! I almost didn't recognize you." He brushed a few chips of plaster off my shoulder before sitting down. "I thought you said you had a few employees working with you now. By the looks of it, though, I would say you are the only one working."

I laughed half-heartedly. "No, I've got four good employees currently working on my hotel venture. I have even hired a bookkeeper. The trouble is, I can't seem to trust my staff. I mean, they aren't as experienced as I am." I told Vern about my issue with the Funar twins and how that reminded me of the issue I had with Tommy a while back. As I was talking, I could see Vern nodding and writing on his notepad. "How can I let them manage themselves if I can't trust them? They just don't understand my goals!"

Vern handed me the sheet of paper. Four phrases were scrawled on it:

1. Differing vision.
2. Poor communication.
3. Personal conflict.
4. Lack of focus and accountability.

"Do you know what these are?" he asked.

I stared blankly at the small sheet and shook my head no.

"These are the four primary factors that will destroy team spirit. Your employees aren't the issue; it is the communication structure you have laid out."

*My fault?* I sat there, staring at Vern's stern look. *What the hell did I do?* "I don't see how communication adds up to me not trusting my employees or vice-versa."

"OK. Effective teams are a hallmark of world-class businesses. A strong culture of teamwork will allow your teams to out-perform and out-innovate any comparable group of individuals. For my first point, it seems like your employees have a different vision of the company, either because it wasn't properly explained to them or properly elaborated on. Effective teams share the same vision and the same objectives. Whether it is the New England Patriots coming together for training camp in the summer with the objective of winning the Super Bowl or a small team in your workplace dedicated to a particular problem, the key is that everyone must have the same goal. And it is your job to both articulate this goal and then to keep communicating it.

"Poor communication will sabotage your teams before they even have a chance to get started. Team members must be able to share feedback and information in a clear and effective manner with one another and with you. For some employees, this isn't a problem. But often good communication skills must be learned—and it is up to you to see that they are.

"Conflict, for any number of reasons, can tear apart a team. Whether it is caused by competition for a promotion or by personal animosity, the conflict will distract and divide your teams. Demand professionalism from your employees as well as yourself, and ensure that they can put aside personal differences to get their job done. If they aren't, you'll need to re-assign them—or perhaps let them go.

"To keep your team engaged, it is important that they have a narrowly defined focus and that they're held accountable. Otherwise, it is easy for any one of them to drift through the workday secure in the knowledge that they aren't personally responsible for anything. Not only does this lead to laziness but it also removes the sense of purpose that is necessary to keep your team working together towards the common goal.

"A team-oriented company can take your business to the next level. But an ineffective team will drag you down; it could ruin you and your business. This may sound dramatic, but time and time again I've seen that this is true. This doesn't just apply to your team; it applies to you as well."

"But I have already butted heads with my team," I said. "I'm worried they distrust me."

"As a manager," replied Vern, "it's inevitable that you'll deal with conflicts between employees from time to time. For one, don't bury your head in the sand—in your case, burying your head in your work. Some part of you believes that if you ignore the problem, it will fix itself. But small interpersonal issues can fester and grow. It is important that you are proactive in resolving conflict before it becomes toxic."

"I know," I replied, "but it seems like things are on the verge of exploding already. How can that be rectified?"

"The best way to get to the bottom of the issue," said Vern, "is to have a conversation with everyone and force them to put their grievances out on the table in plain sight. Many times simply forcing a dialogue between the two parties will lead to a solution without you even doing anything. It is truly astonishing how many conflicts are caused by simple miscommunication or misunderstanding."

"This leads me to my final point: The conflict revolves around your leadership. You may be noticing that your employees feed off your negative attitude, particularly your distrust."

"That may be true," I said, "but when I go in and start talking to them about the issues they have with me, when I attempt to allow two-way communication, it doesn't seem like it's enough. I still have to manage them. I mean, isn't my primary job to manage? Sure I can learn to communicate better—I don't want to alienate my staff, but how am I supposed to manage them and still keep in line with my ultimate goals?"

Vern gave that familiar sigh of exasperation. "Remember, you are not just a manager, you are a leader. In your size business, you have to be both." With a passionate intensity, he wrote on his notepad. He handed me the page, which he had divided into two columns:

| THE MANAGER | THE LEADER |
|---|---|
| Implements the leaders vision & values | Creates the company's vision & values |
| Administrates | Focuses on customers' unmet wants & needs |
| Does things right | Discovers the right things |
| Has a short –term orientation | Has the long-range vision |
| Accepts perceived reality | Asks "How can we_____?" |
| Avoids risk | Manages risk/opportunity |
| Maintains and improves systems | Seeks innovative approaches |
| Creates business structure | Communicates the mission & goals |
| Controls through rules | Focuses on trust and commitment to goals |
| Provides the "how & when" | Provides the "what & why" |
| Takes corrective action | Provides clear direction & expectations |
| Uses incentives | Inspires & empowers |

"Which are you?" he asked.

I looked at the list. "A leader. But I don't think I understand. Given my company's size, can I even do both? Is that even possible? Aren't they inherently contradictory?"

"Hah!" said Vern. "Very good, and perceptive. For many business owners, leadership sounds much more appealing than management. But *both* roles are essential for a business to grow. If you are a natural leader, you need to either hire a good manager or develop the necessary skills yourself. If you are more of a manager, you need to learn the art of leadership. Here are a few things I find useful. For one, document everything. A major issue for many leaders is their ability to *develop* great innovations but their inability to *systematize* them. As a result, the innovations aren't sustainable because they depend on the leader to execute. Begin to groom managers within your organization. You may not be able to hire a full-time manager, but you can develop current employees into capable managers. Look for individuals who are organized and disciplined. Based on what you've told me about Tommy, I think he might have some potential."

"Tommy?" I said. "How could he become a good manager? *I* can't even manage, so how would I teach him? I'm not the kind of guy who can simply be a good manager. I have got enough difficulty organizing my time as it is, especially since I have got to balance my time with trying to come up with new and innovative construction techniques. I can't possibly do all of this. Besides, he screwed up that job a few months back."

"For starters," replied Vern, "Don't artificially limit yourself. I see it time and time again: Many business owners cripple themselves by listening to that voice in their head that says, 'I'm not organized enough to be a good manager' or 'I'm not creative enough to be a good leader.' The only limitations that exist are those you place on yourself—so don't do it. You can learn the skills necessary to be an effective leader."

"Even so," I said, "let's say I allow Tommy to be a manager—even just a short-term manager—and even if I allow myself to 'expand my horizons,' what does that have to do with my employees? They have difficulty engaging, and I have no idea what to do about it. I can't trust them; Everett doesn't have experience, Tommy has made mistakes, and the twins are now ticked at me. Even if I communicate effectively and learn to be this better leader-manager you speak of, how can it matter if I can't trust my own employees?"

Vern scowled, "Haven't you noticed that lack of interest is holding back your employees' buy-in?"

"Buy-in?"

"Yes. It has to do with employee personal interest. It doesn't matter how smart your employees are, or how well you have trained them. If they aren't fully engaged in their work on a daily basis, they won't come close to fulfilling their potential. Engaged employees are emotionally involved in their work. They are constantly asking questions and looking for ways to improve. They solve problems. They innovate.

"In contrast, disengaged employees are bored. They follow directions but don't think for themselves. When stumped by a challenge, they'll look for a way to push the problem onto someone else's desk. They won't invest emotionally in their job. You've seen the symptoms: some of your employees are nervous about proceeding with their work, and if a problem crops up and you are not around to solve it, what do they do? Do they stop work and wait for you? Do they really think and solve the issue for themselves? Do they jump at the first and easiest way to get around it?"

I was starting to feel like I had been shooting myself in the foot. I wasn't sure if I wanted to keep listening to Vern describe all the things I had been doing wrong, but what choice did I have? Even I could tell that my staff was becoming disinterested in their work. "All right," I said, "but how am I supposed to encourage them? How do I turn around the mistakes I've made and the poor management and leadership I've shown?"

By the time I had finished my simple two-sentence question Vern had already drawn up another five points and put them under my nose.

### 5 Steps to Employee Engagement:
1. Give them the freedom to make mistakes.
2. Encourage teamwork.
3. Regularly provide feedback.
4. Seek input.
5. Challenge them.

"Umm, I think I understand," I said, "but could you elaborate a bit more?"

Vern seemed to perk up. "The first thing—and probably the most directly related to your current situation—is to give your employees the freedom to make mistakes. Sure, you can't afford for your team to act recklessly, but allowing them the freedom to make decisions and use their judgment is constructive, even if from time to time it leads to small mistakes that can cost you a little. But mistakes are bound to happen no matter what. Just be sure your employees take corrective action and learn from those mistakes. Reducing your employees to slaves who must never deviate from their script, or micromanaging them into robots, is a sure way to disengage them, ruining both them and you.

"Number two: Encourage teamwork. Working as part of a team will bring out the best in your employees because it makes them accountable to their teammates as well as you. In your case, I think you have a handle on setting up teams and as your business expands keep them working together.

"Three: Provide feedback. Regular feedback lets your employees know that you are paying attention and that you not only care about the work they do but also their thoughts and insights." After pausing to enjoy the last sips of his coffee, he called the waitress over for a refill.

I picked up the conversation. "But those points hinge on me, which I think I can do. The last two points seem more tailored to specific employees and not me as directly."

"It's true," said Vern, "that some employees will give you more input, perhaps more valuable input than others, and some will take on greater challenges, but the process of allowing for input and giving challenges will help drive engagement."

I nodded as he continued in greater detail.

"Always seek input. Asking an employee for his thoughts on a given subject is incredibly empowering. It lets your employee know that you have confidence in him, and it gives him all the more reason to continue to work hard so that he will be prepared to offer valuable insights when the opportunity arises. What you did with your bookkeeper, Lisa, is probably a good example of this. She is trying to develop a website for you using her insight into the details of your marketing and hiring process. Continue to challenge her if she's willing.

"In general, always challenge your employees. Even give them the opportunity to work on a problem that has stumped you. Force them to think outside of their comfort zone. This indicates confidence, and it also keeps their daily routine from becoming monotonous. Think about this: You left your previous job because you couldn't expand your own horizons there. Do you want your employees to do the same?"

That last comment really got to me. "Well, no," I said. "If I had been given a chance to be more creative I might have stayed at Gregory's Building and Housing. I might have still felt some urge to leave, but overall I would have stayed."

"Exactly. Now, what do you think you have to do when you get back to work?"

I saw that Vern was now challenging me. I felt like I was catching on. "Well, I guess I have to communicate my issues with the Funar twins and start giving my employees a bit of leeway. Somehow I'll have to strike a balance between being a good manager and an effective leader while giving my employees the same ability to stretch themselves. I can't limit myself to being only a manager or a leader. I have got to do both."

Vern smiled. He looked at the clock on the wall, then quickly slid his chair back and stood up. "Look at the time! It's been two hours, Jack. I've got to run!" Before turning to leave, he paused and said, "You seem to have good employees. Have a little faith in them and allow them to grow and expand. You might be surprised by what they can accomplish."

Thinking about what I would have to do when I got back to the Colonial Hotel, I was scared. I knew I would have to talk to everyone individually. Part of me wanted to apologize to each of them. I didn't know what it actually took to be a leader-manager, but I figured that, at the very least, I should explain my actions and give them leeway on future projects.

Everett, Daniel, and David were drudging away at the floor when I walked in. None of them seemed at all interested in the project.

"Hey everyone!" I called out.

Everett and David looked up while Daniel kept working.

"Daniel and David, can I speak with you for a moment?" I said.

Together we walked to a private corner of the building. Daniel seemed irritated and avoided eye contact. "Listen," I said, "you guys were right about the wall project—it really is a two-man job. I was so wrapped up and concerned about causing more damage that I convinced myself only I could do the job. But that's not true. You two are skilled carpenters, and I'd like you to finish fixing this hole. Just let me know how you plan on doing it."

Daniel looked up. He seemed interested, and asked in his thick accent, "And if we have more problems?"

"Then you guys solve them. I trust you two. Just keep me apprised. If you feel you need to, you can reach out to me. And if you need Tommy or Everett to assist, just ask them directly. It's fine as long as they can still do their other tasks."

While they both looked bewildered by my change in attitude, I could feel the tension melt away. "We'll have the project done before the end of the work day," said Daniel. David went to gather the necessary tools while Daniel went over the hole and started lining up the job. Daniel had a smile on his face, and they both seemed energized in a way I hadn't seen from either of them before.

*That was easier than I thought.* I surveyed the building; now that I had delegated that task, I had a bit of flexibility about what task I should do next. I saw Everett, sitting in one of the rooms, looking perplexed. I wandered over. "Everett, the flooring work doesn't look done. Are you on break?"

"No, but because you always want someone to supervise me, I figured you'd be pissed if I started working without anyone else around."

Whew, I thought, that's a response right off Vern's notepad! "Listen Everett, you've worked here for a few months, and you've always done a good job. Now is as good a time as any for you to take on projects yourself."

"But I'm not a licensed carpenter," he replied. "I know most of my projects don't require a license, but I always assumed you wanted one of the other licensed guys to check my work."

"Just check in when you're done, Everett, I trust you. If you don't know how to do a particular task, then ask for instruction, either from Tommy or me."

He stared at the moldy floor. I thought he imagined all the ways anything could go wrong. Finally, a sly grin crept onto his face. "I'll let you know when the jobs done."

That day I witnessed a new energy among my employees, and I realized that for the first time in my life I wasn't just *hoping* for success, I was *making it happen*. I wanted to grow my company into an efficient, self-sustaining, and highly profitable business. Even though I knew that goal might be far into the future, I now had a feel for what it would take.

I picked up a notepad and for the first time wrote down my own revelations:

- Identify my objectives.
- What do I hope to get out of my business?
- How much revenue do I want to generate each year?
- How much net income am I hoping for?
- How much time do I want to spend at work?
- Identify the positions I will need to fill to meet my goals.

Right now I had five employees. To meet my long-term goals, I would need to grow my team. In the early days, I had waited until I was overwhelmed before seeking additional help. I was lucky that things worked out, but if I wanted to expand I would soon need more help. What positions will I need to be filled? Whom will I need to hire? And in what order?

I needed to commit to evaluating progress on a weekly basis. It wouldn't be enough just to have a plan. I would need to commit to executing my plan on a regular basis. That would mean setting aside time, each day or, at least, each week, in which I would review my progress and adjust my plan as needed. In the beginning, I didn't have a plan. I had been flying blind—and was lucky. But the odds were that my luck would run out.

I had to *plan for success.*

There was a lot more to do—planning, coordinating, learning—but with this revelation, my first understanding of how to run a business, through all my trials and tribulations, I realized that there was no going back to the way things were. I was not just a business owner but an entrepreneur. I remembered hearing that word "entrepreneur." It seemed purely academic when I first heard it, but now it was real. The difference between being an entrepreneur and a business owner was in the degree to which one identified, sourced, and organized resources and people, including oneself. I had thought I only wanted to be a business owner, but I was taking my first steps in being an entrepreneur.

# Chapter 6
## THE TEAM

T he cold days of winter led to the humid days of spring. I was used to it, though, and as I worked on job sites, the beads of sweat on my back streamed down like drops of water off a duck. Sure, I didn't like the humidity, but at this point, I was more concerned about our epoxy and paint not setting properly.

Even though I had instituted new systems into Jack's Modern Design that had helped us expand significantly, including a new website and a refined hiring process, I still had to toil many more hours than I would have liked. Unfortunately, whenever I wrote down my goals, working less never seemed to fit into my ninety-day schedule. It was my goal for the end of the year, but it never seemed within reach. Despite taking on Tommy as a part-time manager, we frequently found ourselves trying to juggle more than either of us knew how. The biggest issue was that I had taken on another office assistant for Lisa, and, with the new website, we got more phone calls than I could have imagined. The number of proposals I went out on jumped, but half of these fell through because we weren't the cheapest firm. So I tried to focus our advertising more on getting customers who were interested in specialized design. In the meantime, the company still needed someone to take those calls and make those estimates.

On top of doing proposals, we had tons of extra jobs. This meant I needed more staff, so I hired an additional two carpenters and an electrician. Hiring an electrician was a necessity, but now I felt I needed to learn some of the basics of electrical contracting to be better informed and properly manage one. Even though I could have used someone's help on the very day the prospects came in for their interviews, I had learned my lesson about hiring, though, and I took my time making a decision. Out of the twenty or so people I interviewed, only three seemed to click with our mentality.

Learning about an electrician's work was just the tip of the iceberg regarding my workload. Some days my teams were working at two or three separate locations. With Tommy as only a part-time manager, I frequently had to drive from location to location to keep an eye on things. Even worse, some days, to keep work on schedule, I found myself having to get my hands dirty. I knew I would soon need a full-time manager. I was spread too thin, and on some days, even Tommy looked exhausted. I was getting good at multitasking, but how effectively or efficiently was another matter.

This became obvious on one particular long workday at the hotel job.

We had nearly completed the exterior and had installed color-changing lights that would faintly and gradually change the color of the white exterior without being overbearing. We had also started cleaning up the interior, going room by room. Most of the work had been fairly tedious and routine. However, our client asked for a new addition to the roof. He also wanted a massive outdoor infinity-edge pool with a swim-up bar. These seemed simple enough, but he wanted an entirely retractable/extendable roof and glass walls so that during the winter the setting became an indoor area sufficiently heated to maintain a balmy temperature. It took me over a month, working with a structural engineer, to determine the proper materials for the roof and heating units alone, let alone test the structure to make sure it was sturdy enough to endure the additional weight.

The project seemed formidable, and I had to come up with new and relatively untested ideas. Everett had model-making skills, so I had him work a few hours every day on some functional designs. Between the two of us, we had gathered fifteen separate materials just to build a working model, and all but two were shot down by our client. Even while I was developing these models with Everett, we still had other jobs to work. I still got emails from potential clients; I still had to check on the work at another project across town—work, work, work. Sometimes I would have to set down my phone just so I could focus on the task at hand, but then ring, ring, ring.

"Yes, Carl, I'll take a look at the lighting."

"Yes, David, I'll come across town and take a look at your work, but isn't Tommy there right now?" (No, he had to tend to an emergency for his wife.) "Fine, I'll be there in ten!"

"Hold on Lisa, I'll take a look at the website update in a minute. Can you please change the colors, we are not that rustic, get rid of the green and browns, find something more modern."

As the calls continued, I would be dragged off to new sites. By the time I started to work on the newest project, I would be called away to the next thing.

I felt like couldn't ignore any call because they all seemed urgent.

At the end of the day, I was accomplishing very little. I was just hopping between sites, between tasks, and between each employee on every single task.

*No more! No more!* I knew I was becoming less and less productive with each new task.

Then one day at the hotel I wondered, *What if I just turned off my phone?* The job across town could survive without me; they were just doing simple work. I had been working on the model with Everett for the better part of two weeks now and wanted to get it done. What if I just focused on that, without interruption? I did, and, without the phone or email or other miscellaneous tasks to distract me, we assembled the model and got it almost entirely working. I was amazed at how much more effective I became when I just focused on one task.

After a few hours, I turned my phone back on. To my surprise, there had been no emergencies! There were a few emails from crews telling me they were nearing completion on a few jobs across town, and I would need to inspect their work. But why should it be me? When I got the chance to buckle down on tasks, I seemed to be able to not only work more effectively but with far more ingenuity. The vision I had laid forth could not be accomplished if I was multitasking all day. I noticed that my time was my most valuable resource, yet it was my worst enemy when I spent it on tasks that could be done by others. I pulled out my notebook and wrote down a few points I thought would allow me to better spend my time.

✓ Start each week, month, and year by setting priorities.

Sure, there would always be times when I would have to remain flexible and deal with some customer or other semi-emergencies, but if I lost focus on the big picture, I would just wind up working longer and harder without getting anything done.

✓ Avoid multitasking whenever possible.

This seemed obvious to me at this point, but I figured I should keep a note of it. Some days I might have to do a bit of multitasking, but it seemed clear that when I focused on a single tasks until it was done, I was far more productive.

✓   Don't let email, or phone calls, dictate how I spend my time.

This tied directly into multitasking. Certainly email and my phone were the biggest offenders. Scheduling "interruption-free" blocks of time throughout my day—preferably for several hours at a time—made me much more productive.

✓   Give myself time to reflect, relax, and refocus. Spend more time with my family.

From the time I woke up until the time I went to bed at night, I was constantly on the move. It was all business, all the time. This had to be unhealthy, and it was also ineffective. My mind and body needed time to relax and recharge.

This was going to be a challenge. I had to manage many sites at a time, and too many things needed my personal attention, even on weekends.

I decided that because we would soon regularly have two or three projects going at any given time, and emergencies would still happen, I needed to hire a project manager.

But could I afford one?

I gave Lisa a call and asked her to work on an online post for a project manager. At the very least, I could find out if anyone was interested.

Maybe, too, my friend Vern would have some insight.

I sent him an email. For the first time, I was capable of including some lessons I had discovered for myself. In the email, I told him about my discoveries in time management and how I had learned to resist the temptation of pulling out my phone every few minutes to check for emails and phone calls. I asked him if I was on the right track in looking to hire a project manager, and if so, what qualities to look for in one.

The rest of that day I spent helping set up the slide rails for the retractable roof. Even though I was eager for Vern's response, I kept my vow and didn't turn my phone on while we finished the job. And we made astonishing progress. I hadn't expected to get all the rails set up before the end of the day, but we did. Then I checked my email.

Vern had sent me several messages. The first one related to what I had to say about time management.

*Dear Jack,*

*I am very proud of you; it's good to see you making revelations for yourself, especially with regards to time management. Even for myself, I find it particularly difficult to set time aside to dedicate to just one task. I think I can add some additional points to what you discovered. These have helped me find success over the years.*

*Want to get more done? Spend your time only doing what you are good at!*

*Take a moment to make a list of the five business functions that you are best at.*

*Once you are done, look over your list. Now, estimate how much of your workday you spend on these functions.*

*If you spend 50% or more of your day working in these areas, you are in good shape. And, I'm willing to venture, you are enjoying your job and doing quite well from a business standpoint. Why? Because it is human nature to enjoy what we are good at. It feels good to be productive. It is rewarding to complete challenging projects successfully. And when we spend time leveraging our strengths, our business benefits.*

*But many business owners that I know spend maybe 10% or less of their time each day working in the areas where they are most gifted. In most of these cases, the individual does not enjoy going to work each day. Often, the business is struggling to make ends meet—and even if it is profitable, it is not even close to achieving its potential.*

Here are three simple steps that will help you spend more time leveraging your strengths.

1.  *Make time for what you are good at. Particularly for your business, one that is relatively small, there is no getting around the other responsibilities. In your case, the only way to spend time on your areas of expertise is to devote additional time before or after the workday, or on the weekends. While this may not sound appealing, it is worth it for a short while, because it will allow your business to grow, which brings us to step two.*

2.  *Find employees who can free you. If your core strengths relate to marketing, hire an employee who can focus on operations. Often, business owners hire employees similar to themselves. You should be doing the opposite—hire someone who is strong in areas where you are weak. When you are looking for a manager, keep this in mind.*

3.  *Create systems that allow you to work more effectively. I know that you and I both can be overwhelmed with everyday work, which keeps us from focusing on our strengths. Often, we approach this work in a haphazard manner, which only makes it last longer. Take the time to create systems for managing daily work, and devote the time that you save to the work that you are uniquely best at.*

The more time you can spend each day utilizing your strengths, the happier you will be, and the better off your business will be. It is a win-win proposition.

Best,

Vern

I wondered how much time I spent on the things I loved to do. Up until today, very little! I let the smallest, insignificant, and tedious projects get in the way.

What did I love to do? I loved architecture. I loved working on models and bringing the real thing to in existence. I enjoyed researching new ideas for my projects. I enjoyed going to new sites and seeing how I could apply new concepts. I didn't mind managing and doing the work, but that was mostly tedious.

It seemed obvious that I needed an operations manager.

Then I read the second email from Vern. The subject line was "Winning Teams."

*Dear Jack,*

*Now that I have whetted your appetite, I assume you are still wondering how to hire a manager. But what do managers actually manage? Winning teams. If you don't have a productive team, your business will never reach its full potential.*

*When looking for a manager, you must know the qualities of a winning team and chose the manager to be the leader of that team.*

*There are three primary aspects of winning teams both you and your manager will have to cultivate in order to build them.*

1. *Build a winning team by setting standards and defining expectations.*

   *There's a lot that goes into managing a team of employees. But sometimes, especially when you are busy, it is easy to overlook the obvious. And I can't tell you how many business owners and managers alike overlook this critical first step in creating effective teams.*

   *Many business owners admit that their employees don't have clearly defined roles and responsibilities. But* this presents a major problem. How are your employees supposed to meet and exceed your expectations if they don't know what they are?

Far too many business owners expect their employees to "figure it out" by themselves, to work together to make sure all critical objectives are achieved. And while this sounds great in theory, the real world tells us that if responsibility isn't directly assigned, important tasks often go uncompleted.

If you haven't already done so, it is important that you take the time to define the roles and responsibilities of each position within your organization. I call these "position agreements." Assign specific responsibilities to each position in your business, and make sure those responsibilities are clearly communicated to each employee. Any manager you hire who oversees a project will have to be able to do the same.

2. Make sure that your employees have both the resources and the knowledge needed to meet their responsibilities. This is where many business owners go off course: They assign responsibility but fail to give their employees the resources and the authority to accomplish their goals. This is demoralizing for your employees and fatal to your organization. Don't simply assign responsibility; take the time to ensure that your employees are in a position to meet your expectations. Many managers have the tendency to view their employees as robots who can master any task. They get so focused on getting the job done that they don't look to see if their employees have the necessary resources and knowledge. A culture of openness is important too; the manager should never be afraid to approach you if

*there's an issue. Make sure a manager can communicate a concern if they think they can't acquire the resources and knowledge themselves.*

3. *Help your employees see the "big picture." Help them see how their job ties into the larger picture of your business, and how they interact with other members of your team. Help them see the purpose behind their daily work and understand how their job impacts the effectiveness of the team as a whole. Make sure any manager you choose sees your big picture and can effectively communicate it as well.*

   *Employees need to know the chain of command and how their work is directed. You can't just throw ten people in a room and expect them to figure out how to get the job done. Every boss or manager has the job of assigning each person a specific role and then giving them the resources they need to perform. This is how teams become more productive and more effective.*

4. *Build a winning team by putting your people in the position to succeed.*

   *Any good leader must be able to put their people in a position to succeed.*

   *It may sound easy and obvious, but I can't tell you how often business owners don't stay true to this principle.*

   *Think about football for a moment. For a team to be successful, a group of players with very different skills must work together. On offense, you need several players with overwhelming strength in order to block the defense. You need players with the ability to run with the ball effectively. You need a quarterback to lead the unit and to make decisions while handling the football.*

*It is critical that you and your manager understand that each employee is unique. To maximize the value that each employee provides to your company, you must put them in a position to best use their unique skills and abilities. Neither you nor your manager should try to make a pass receiver perform as an offensive lineman!*

*Keep this question in mind when you are hiring: Would you rather hire a really good team player to whom you can teach your method or someone with an impressive résumé but who you don't think will fit in with the team? Of course, you need someone who's qualified, but you also need an employee who's going to enthusiastically help your organization move ahead. Likewise, when you hire a manager, make sure you hire someone who has room to grow and a capacity for growth, and not just someone stuck in their way of doing things.*

*As a business owner and manager, you'll need your team to take your business where you want it to go. You want a manager who puts your employees in positions that match up well with their skills. Doing so will help them to feel happier and more fulfilled, and it will allow you to maximize the value they provide to your business.*

5. *Build a winning team by developing your workforce.*

*So far, I have discussed the importance of clearly defining the responsibilities of each member of your team and of ensuring that you assign the right people to the right positions. It is a task you and any manager you hire must share. While these steps will help create an effective and productive team, they're only part of the battle. A good manager must also develop the team by helping them grow both individually and as a unit.*

*How do you make this growth happen? By providing feedback and by providing the training each employee needs to improve.*

*It is important that you and any manager take the time to regularly provide feedback and further training to each employee. I highly recommend taking the time to review each employee's performance on a regular basis, not just once or twice per year. Why? Because otherwise your employees are flying blind. A good rule to follow is to communicate frequently and candidly so that there are no surprises.*

*Providing regular feedback is critical, but it is only half of the equation. It is not enough for you or a manager to tell your employees where they need to improve. If you expect to truly get the most out of each team member, you need to provide the training necessary to help them achieve their growth goals. This may mean sales training, it may mean attending management seminars, or it may mean communication workshops with your manager. Whatever the case may be, the point is that you need to give your employees and your managers the tools they require to continue their development. Otherwise, it is not going to happen!*

*Investing resources to train employees and managers who already have the ability to get their job done may seem like an expense that doesn't provide a return, but it is not. The truth is that the productivity and the effectiveness of your team play a huge role in determining the overall success of your business. Don't sell yourself short. Help each member of your workforce reach his or her full potential.*

*Keep in mind that any manager is a reflection of you. Make sure whoever you choose maintains your vision, communicates effectively, and maintains winning teams. Keep this in mind and you will be all right.*
*Best of luck,*
*Vern*

It seemed like my preconceptions about management were wrong. Instead of micromanaging, good management was about fostering and maintaining a productive, fulfilled, winning team that could function without me. The challenge for me was that I needed someone who would understand and support my company's culture. How could I go out and hire a manager and be sure he or she embraced my vision?

I figured that when I started screening managers, I would have to discover their understanding of my vision. Vern had highlighted this, so I figured it would be the key quality I should be looking for. I knew it wouldn't be something I could find in just a résumé; I would need to thoroughly interview each candidate.

Within a week of the job being posted, Lisa had managed to gather five suitable candidates. Two had MBAs as carpenters, and three were long-time licensed carpenters who had been managers in their previous firms. I set aside some time to meet with each of them at a small French café down the road from the hotel project.

Entering the café, the aroma of sweet, freshly baked croissants made my stomach growl—but since I was trying to watch my waistline I resisted the temptation. I took a seat and began reviewing the résumé of my first candidate, Brian, an older gentleman who spent the better part of his early career as a form carpenter. When he was in his forties, he had been promoted to project supervisor. He listed a number of separate projects he had overseen; they usually involved teams of three to seven men. He seemed like a good candidate.

The little bell on the door let me know that someone had just entered the quiet café. I looked up. A stocky, wind-blown man was standing in the doorway. Must be Brian, I thought, as I waved him over to the seat across from me.

He introduced himself and sat down.

"I was just going through your credentials," I said, "and you have certainly had your fair share of supervising projects. I was a bit curious as to your insight about how you have led your teams to success?"

He seemed mystified by my question and sat there a minute before responding. "That's certainly not the kind of question I'm used to. Usually, people just want to know the nitty-gritty details of the jobs. Well, let's see. Usually, I try first to make sure I have the right qualified people for the task at hand. It would be ridiculous to even attempt any task without making sure you have the proper people." He then went into detail about making sure his people had the right resources for the jobs and that they were working on time and on schedule. He even surprised me by saying he wanted continuous feedback on each of his employees' tasks.

He seemed to have a solid grasp of winning teams. Now I just needed to know if he could understand my vision. I asked, "Brian, if I may, how do you feel about using new carpentry techniques and ideas, even those you are unfamiliar with, and trying to learn and develop their uses within any given project?"

"Well, new things are fine and well, but I much prefer methods that are tried and true. I mean, why fix something if it isn't broke?"

After a few more minutes of conversation I got the impression that while he was qualified, he was set in his ways and not very flexible. I thought to myself, *scratch one candidate.*

I thanked Brian for his time. I had four other candidates waiting; I was sure that one of them would pan out.

I couldn't have been more wrong. Each one had something lacking: either they were too stuck in their ways to be able to understand my vision or they couldn't grasp winning teams. One of them even said he didn't care about his employees, just whether or not the project got done! It was exactly what Vern had warned me about. I couldn't afford to have someone bring their old ways that could subvert mine. I decided not to follow up with any of the candidates.

I made my way back to the hotel job site. I was surprised to see Tommy's car out front; today wasn't a day he normally worked. Maybe he was trying to squeeze in a bit of overtime? Entering the hotel, I saw Tommy near the entrance, he looked up, "Hey Jack, there's something I have meant to talk to you about. My wife is doing better and doesn't need me to be around the house to help out as much. You know I could use the extra money, and since we still need a few extra hands, I was wondering if I could come on as a full-time carpenter."

"It's a possibility," I said. "We could use the extra hands." *Hold on a second*, I thought to myself. Why was I going out to find a new manager when Tommy had already proven himself as a part-time project manager? "Tommy," I said, "do you still have our company beliefs in your pocket?"

"Yup," he tapped his jacket pocket. "Right here."

"Tommy, how would you like to be our full-time operations manager? You've proven yourself capable of leading our teams productively, and you know our beliefs. What do you say?"

Tommy stared at his shoes. The look on his face made it seem he was battling something in his mind. I wondered if he felt this was too big a step. Finally, he looked up and spoke, "Well, I have never managed full-time before. I don't even know if I will like it. It seems like a lot of responsibility, but I think I could do it. Just let me know what you need me to do and I'll keep you posted."

*Yes!* Why didn't I see it before? Tommy was who I was looking for—someone who understood my vision, who time and time again proved himself working in teams, and who could learn from mistakes. Sure, he would need a bit of grooming to get used to the role, but it would give both of us the practice we would need for communicating with each other and giving practical feedback.

To me, this was the next big step for my business. With Tommy as operations manager, I could finally dedicate more time to the creative and innovative aspects of my business. Through effective time management and winning teams coming together, it seemed like no obstacles could keep me from reaching my goals.

# Chapter 7
# THE MISCREANT ADOLESCENT

●━━━━━━━━━━━━━━━━━●

With Tommy working full time and managing teams on other projects, everything I could have ever hoped for seemed to be coming together. Tommy needed a few weeks to get the swing of managing, and to help him I shared much of Vern's material on how to create winning teams. Together, we learned to establish an effective dialogue between ourselves and individual team members. He seemed to enjoy working with me on my ideas about bettering our teams; after all, we both wanted winning teams. But we struggled with the best way to deliver effective feedback that wouldn't alienate our team members.

This became an issue as we were wrapping up the hotel project. I was off scouting a new job and was offsite most of that day. A few minor touch-ups on the pool had to be done, and Everett and Carl were working on installing an "in-room scent generator," a specialized device built into the ventilation system that allowed an occupant to press a button and change the aroma in the room. The main problem facing them was that the unit was so bulky that it protruded out of the wall into each room like a hideous window AC unit.

The problem arose when Carl complained that the task was impossible without gutting a portion of the wall and starting from scratch. The two argued nonstop for a few hours before Tommy came down from the pool to check on them. According to Tommy's email to me, things went south quickly, and then something he said fixed it:

*Hey Jack,*

*Just a quick update on the in-room scent generator project you had Everett and Carl working on.*

*The two of them were going ballistic at each other. Carl was furious because to run the electric power lines for the generator they would have to tear apart parts of the wall, which he didn't want to do. Everett then got angry at him about losing sight of the project and that they would fail if they didn't tear apart the wall. At first, I told them just to calm down and stop arguing and get it done. Two hours later I come back down to see Everett tearing apart the wall and Carl missing. I finally found Carl in the parking lot. He was steaming that no one appreciated the work he had to do with learning how to install all these brand new systems he has never worked with before, and that no one ever followed-up with him during the construction work to see how it would affect the electrical side of things.*

*After he had finished, I sat down with him and told him about the good work he was doing. I told him that if there was an issue with a project that he should immediately come to me (or you, if I wasn't around). I explained to him that ripping up a few bits of drywall wasn't a big deal if it is what it took to get the job done properly.*

*I explained that I would try harder to follow up with him and that in the future he should let me know if he saw any glaring construction issues that interfered with any of his work.*

*Carl seemed satisfied with what I told him. He went back to work with Everett, and they both understand they'll have to tear up the drywall a bit to get those units properly installed.*

*Just keeping you informed! Tommy*

I was pleasantly surprised how Tommy had given such effective feedback and had kept me in the loop. Tommy had established a proper feedback system that I would be able to adopt. His job and my job were to point out the areas that needed improvement and to encourage, motivate, and guide each employee as they worked to be the best they could be.

Below are five key takeaways that came to mind from this episode:

1. Keep it brief. There was no reason to drag the conversation on longer than it had to be. Tommy made his point, made sure Carl understood, and then they got on with their day.

2. Keep it positive. Even as Tommy addressed the problem with Carl's performance and attitude, he kept the tone positive. Tommy explained that Carl was valuable to the organization and had lots of potential. If he hadn't said this, Carl might have walked away discouraged.

3. Keep it clear. Don't beat around the bush. Focus only on the behavior that needs to change. Explain how it needs to change, why it needs to change, and what the appropriate behavior looks like. Make it about the behavior, not about the person. Tommy didn't overcomplicate things!

4. Keep it private. This might have happened because Carl had walked out to the parking lot, but regardless of the circumstances,

never, ever, deliver negative feedback in public. Even if it wouldn't seem like a big deal to Tommy or me, the experience of being negatively singled out in front of co-workers or customers can be extremely damaging to an employee. Also, it could be bad for the morale of the entire team and it could weaken their trust in me. How could my team be expected to innovate and take chances if they worried about public humiliation?

5. Follow up. This is an inevitable next step Tommy would have to take. The feedback session couldn't be the end; it had to be the start of a process. We would have to closely monitor Carl's performance, and not just him but the entire team. If Carl did a good job of addressing the issue that had been raised, he would be commended for it. If not, we would need to let him know that he needed to make more progress—and we would have to make sure he had the tools and the knowledge he needed to do so.

I was very proud to have Tommy as a manager. It seemed like he could prevent small problems from turning into large fires that I would then have to put out. As I pulled up to a point overlooking the location of our next big job, I breathed more easily.

I had been told very little about this new job, only that our future client had heard good references and thought that our work sounded particularly useful for building his summer home overlooking a beautiful lake in New Hampshire. The tiny peninsula was like a fragrant, refreshing oasis of tranquility. In the distance, a lone mountain rose up over the water, and I could see the clear grass strips that must have been intended for skiing. But where was the house?

I looked around. This certainly seemed like the area my client had described, but there was no house. After a few minutes, I heard the sound of gravel crunching under the wheels of an approaching car. I turned to see a red Bentley driving up the road and then parking in front of my little Nissan. A tall, well-built, stern looking man got out of the car. His expression softened as he walked over.

"Well I'm glad you found the place," he said. "It took the crew that cleared away the trees an hour to find the place before they had to call me. I should have realized then they would be nothing but trouble. They practically destroyed this entire peninsula, digging up the roots. I nearly fired them for their idiotic style. By the way, name's Chris. Chris Corro." He extended his hand.

As we shook hands I thought, *Chris Corro*. I had heard that name somewhere—possibly on the radio. "Mr. Corro," I said, "I know that name and yet I don't think we've met—"

"Ha!" He cut me off. "I take it you don't listen to a lot of country music. Yep, you've heard of me; I've got a string of top ten country songs. They paid for this Bentley, and they're going to pay for this house. Ordinarily I might be tempted to judge you by your music choice, but I've seen some of your work first hand. That is why I want to hire you."

"First hand?" I asked, a bit confused. "Which building?"

"Well, there were two that caught my attention. There was a housing development up by Mallord Street a friend of mine was looking at. He said the houses were nice, but what really stood out to him was the day room that converted into a theater! I've certainly heard about room conversion, but not quite to this extent; so I did a bit of research and found out about your company, JMD."

*JMD? What's he talking about?* I thought. *Oh—Jack's Modern Design. Could make a cool logo.*

"So what did you find out about us?" I asked.

"When I dug into it, I mean most of your projects seemed normal, still well done, but then I found out about that hotel project. That's when I became interested. I heard about how you managed to convert an outdoor pool into an indoor pool. Amazing! Not only once, but twice you turned a mundane single use room into something that could be used in several ways! I scouted a few people in the area, but twice your work stood out, I had to have you as my builder!"

I wondered if my work actually stood out that much, was I doing something unique, did my dream actually matter to people? It all seemed too good to be true. "So what is it you are looking for?" I asked. "I mean, when I came here, I was expecting to see a house or, at least, a basic structure to work with."

"Ha!" he laughed. "If everyone hadn't been so incompetent then there might have been a finished house here. I did have an architect for the house who was working on a design, but I didn't like his attitude or his narrow-mindedness. He kept telling me how things *couldn't* be done. The first batch of carpenters did the same. I figured based, on your experience, it wouldn't matter for you. What I want is for you to repeat your past, innovative style of work and create a multidimensional home for me. I want nearly every single room to morph in some way. I want my summer home to *pop*."

Jeez, I thought, this guy is tough, firing people for attitude issues. Sure I could understand the reasons behind it, but from what I heard, he had fired three groups of people. Maybe they weren't the best hires he could have chosen, but it was clear to me that this guy had strict standards. "So you want JMD to build your entire house? I mean, I'll need to work with you about what you'll want the house to have room-wise and how it will look aesthetically—"

"Fine, fine," he interrupted. "We'll discuss all that later, but I'm not hearing you complaining, so you've got the job. Also, I need everything built in the next nine months, give or take a bit. I would like to be moved in by next summer."

Only nine months! We would have to work around the clock to accomplish that. As we finished discussing terms for our agreement, my mind raced as I wondered how JMD could pull off this ambitious project.

Later that day I gathered the team to fill them in on the deal and what was at stake. Everyone was enthusiastic. Apparently Chris Corro was a big-name country singer, and many of the staff were excited about not only possibly meeting him but about personally building his home.

Only Tommy expressed concern when I mentioned the time frame. "Jack, even on our best of days, pulling off this deadline would be difficult, but now you are adding an hour, even an hour and a half extra driving time for many of our guys. That will significantly cut into our labor times."

"Don't worry Tommy," I said, "some of the labor will be handled by a local group; our guys won't be too strapped. We only need to work on the specialized projects." Despite my assurances, there was the look of deep concern in Tommy's eyes. He and I both knew most of the jobs on this house would be specialized and that we would still have to work around the clock.

But this job was bigger than JMD: this job was my chance to shine, to build a home for a celebrity! It would last for years and make it into the papers. My name would become known. Who cared if a few of our guys had to pull extra hours? I had been doing that for years. Now was my time to be in the limelight.

After a few weeks of hammering out details with Chris, the vacation home project finally started. I quickly realized that outsourcing part of the work to a cheaper firm gave us both greater flexibility and saved our time for the more expensive specialized aspects of the job. The first job I outsourced was laying the foundation and pouring the concrete for the beginning part of the structure. My guys could have done it in the same amount of time, but it would have drawn them away from finishing the hotel project.

I began applying this principle across the board. I had even hired an online freelance web designer to help Lisa. JMD finally got up and running on the internet.

I told Vern about my discovery during a phone call.

"Outsourcing some of our labor seems to have taken our systems to the next level," I told him. "Whether it is freelancers or specialty firms, outsourcing has led to enhanced effectiveness for JMD's systems—and improved the level of the services we offer to our customers. I began to realize this when I asked myself a simple question: Which systems and what type of work should I outsource? The answer was simple: Any work that could be done more efficiently or less costly outside of JMD!"

"Yes!" Vern said. "Outsourcing can lead to great things. In fact, I frequently outsource parts of my required labor. For instance, I took over a small plumbing company a few years back, but none of the staff was an effective marketer. I directed the CEO to look around and outsource their marketing to an online freelancer. Outsourcing in my furniture business allowed us to expand the list of products we offered. In the beginning, we only offered simple wooden furniture, and then we hired a metal fabrication company to build modern designs."

In the course of a month, outsourcing gave JMD the ability to tackle multiple projects with ease. We almost doubled our operation. We had time to finish the hotel project to a top standard, and we got our ducks in line to begin the Corro project.

Once the Corro project was underway, Tommy's concerns proved to be right: the long drive was taking its toll on our staff. Even so, no one seemed to lose enthusiasm for the job. Everyone's passion drove them to work the hardest and the best I had seen. But I couldn't let them screw this up; it was too important to me... I mean to JMD.

We were setting the basement to allow for an easy transition between a home theater and a game room. Most of the electronic gaming systems could be directly linked to the big screen, but we also wanted to allow for a drop-away foosball table and for pinball machines that popped in and out of the walls. While we weren't yet to the point of installing any machines, we needed to build the structural supports for the entire building that would allow for these systems to tuck away. Tommy, the twins, and Everett were slowly building the supports. We were using a steel alloy that was fifty percent more durable than most structural supports. Fitting the metal into place and drilling it was taking a lot of time and energy.

One afternoon I approached the group. "So you guys think you can get this done before heading off for the day?"

Daniel looked up. "You kidding? We'll be lucky to get most of them done, but the final few will take tomorrow."

"Come on guys," I said, "we need to get this done today. We're starting to drift off schedule, and we need to lay the supports upstairs. I want the basement set and done today!"

"We'll have to be here almost two extra hours," David interjected. "We won't get home until eight or nine o'clock!"

Tommy approached me and said, "Can I talk to you in private?"

We went outside and stood overlooking the lake. Tommy's face looked stern. "These guys have families to get back to. Just give them a break. Everett woke up at five o'clock to get here by seven so that he could make sure the new supports would fit. The twins weren't far behind. These guys just can't work twelve-hour days; they're not robots."

"Well," I paused, thinking that because I wanted the project done, I might have started losing perspective—but no, it had to get done. This was my dream.

I made up a story. "Chris is calling for a status update tomorrow. If you want to explain to him that we haven't even finished setting up the basement supports, go ahead. Just get the project done. We don't want to end up like the other three contractors he hired and then promptly fired!"

Tommy scanned my face. He squinted. I wondered if he sensed I was lying "Fine," he said, "I'll let the guys know we have to get this done tonight."

Whoever said honesty was the best policy? *Results* were what mattered. I now had a go-to response to get the guys having to work late: whenever someone complained about having to work late, I just let them know that Chris would be checking in and that they would have to explain our lack of progress.

Little did I know that lying spreads like the plague.

After weeks of making similar threats, I could see the long days wearing on everyone. The passion they once had vanished and was replaced by looks of anguish whenever I told them about the coming days' and weeks' projects. But they kept working away—until they decided to imitate my tactics.

"Hey, boss!" Daniel and David called me over. "Listen," David said, "we just got off the phone with our sister, and she's recovering from surgery on her—"

"Knee!" Daniel jumped in.

"Yes, her knee. Anyway, she needs some help at home and doing groceries and the like, so we won't be able to work past three most days. That won't be a problem, will it?"

I noticed Everett look up. Was he holding back a snicker? "Very well," I said. "Family must come first, I guess."

The twins bolted to the door, "Thanks, Jack!" I watched their car driving away down the dirt road, trailing a plume of dust.

Over the next few weeks, the twins kept leaving early. Our projects dragged on as slow as molasses. To make things worse, Everett had started having "car troubles," and was arriving to work later and later. The twelve-hour days they used to pull suddenly shrunk to five- and six-hour days. Tommy and I had to pick up the slack. We worked more and more hours. Finally, I snapped.

"Tommy, why haven't you reeled in our guys yet? They keep working less and less—and not even that productively—leaving me to do all the work!"

"You? Ha!" Tommy said, red in the face. "You're doing all the work? Bull! I'm here busting my rear as much as you and you expect me to reel in the guys after you drove them off! I have tried to maintain their spirits, but everyone knows you are lying about Chris checking in on you; after all, it has been all over the freaking news that he's on some safari in Africa and is completely out of touch with the rest of the world! You lied to them. You drove them like mules! And you have the audacity to blame me for their behavior?"

"But—"

"Look. You've done right by me, and overall you've been a good boss. But your behavior on this project is making almost all of us want to quit. Everett's been digging around for other work, and the twins are just biding their time until they see a new opportunity as well. To be fair, I think you deserve another chance. But unless *you* start using the systems you instructed me to use, consider this my two weeks' notice."

I let out a heavy sigh. "Tommy—"

"Jack, you used to ask for feedback. We still try to give it to you, but you just dismiss us. You used to be truthful and honest with us, and now you lie to make deadlines. You used to view us as people, now you seem to view us as some sort of drill bit, use it until it burns out and breaks. Unless you start treating us like people again, I quit. And Everett and the twins will probably follow."

He packed up his equipment. He had the most defeated look I have ever seen on a man. But what could I say?

"I'll see you tomorrow, Jack," Tommy said as he walked away.

I had nothing to say. My gut wrenched. After so much progress how could I have so quickly regressed? I had to talk to Vern.

On my long drive home, I called Vern. It went straight to voicemail. Damn. I really needed him. I left a message.

"Hey, Vern, it's Jack. Listen, I've got a big problem at work." I went into detail about the lies I had told and how productivity was suffering since I pushed my guys too hard. I spent so much time talking that I had to leave a second voice mail. "I just don't understand it. I was trying to make things more productive, but it almost ruined me. I could lose my operations manager and half my staff!"

When I arrived home, Erica greeted me with a cheery grin that lifted my spirits for a second. Her smile faded, though, when she saw how distraught I was. I told her what happened. She tried to help by saying, "Jack, you are a good man. Tommy has said so. You two will work it out." I wish I could have shared her optimism.

I couldn't sleep that night. Tommy's words ravaged my brain. Had I been so consumed by my ego that I nearly sacrificed my entire business and drove good employees to do bad things? I don't know how long I tossed and turned in bed before I heard the beeping noise of an incoming email. It was three o'clock. The message was from Vern.

*Hey Jack,*

*I am sorry to hear about your troubles. I wish I could speak to you directly, but I am currently out of the country. As for what you did wrong, I think, in your heart, you know it to be true, and you even said it yourself: you lied, and you treated your employees like robots. Let's explore your first issue and how you can rectify it.*

*Honesty Is the Best Policy:*

*Can you trust your employees? Can they trust you? Can they trust each other?*

*If you can truthfully answer each of those questions with a "yes," I'm willing to bet that you are going to be successful. But* now you can't say "yes." You used to be able to, and things were going well.

Trust is a critical component of every effective team and every organization, but it is rare in the world of business today. You are not the first to lie to your staff to try to increase productivity. But how can you recreate a culture of honesty in your business? Here are four ideas:

1.  Promote open communication, even when it is hard. An honest culture is not necessarily peaceful all of the time. Whether or not your employees are honest, they are still going to have problems with each other, with management, and with you from time to time.

    Encourage your employees to speak their minds— respectfully and constructively, of course. When employees feel that their co-workers, their managers, and you will listen to their opinions, honesty becomes second nature.

2.  Create alignment between your goals and the goals of your employees. Dishonesty happens when employees and managers have different objectives. Articulate your goals and give your employees reason to buy into your mission. When you and your team are working for the same goals, honesty happens naturally.

3.  Set the example. As usual, the onus is on you as the business owner to set the tone. By providing honest feedback to your team, and by communicating openly with them, even if the news is bad, you will inspire them to do the same. On the other hand, if you are only honest when it suits your purposes, do not expect any more than that from your team. And if you lie to them, expect that they will lie to you, too.

4. *Trust is a big deal. Teams that trust their leaders and trust each other are willing to take risks, willing to innovate, willing to try new things. If that trust doesn't exist, employees are more likely to cover their butts than think outside the box. When there's no trust in your organization, you are not as effective, and it will infect every element of your organization. That's the bottom line.*

I looked up from the email. I had done just the opposite for the past few months. I would have to cultivate trust again, but how could I if my employees wouldn't want to come back? I continued to read.

*Your people aren't robots.*

*Owning a business has plenty of advantages, but business ownership also brings with it unique challenges. It is great to be the boss. In fact, when entrepreneurs are dreaming of starting their own business, being the boss is often a primary motivation. It was true for you, wasn't it?*

*But with that exciting job description come challenges that many entrepreneurs never envisioned—namely, the reality that if you mismanage your employees, the results can be catastrophic, which is what you are witnessing first hand.*

*Let's review the basic concepts that are essential to your success as a manager.*

*You need to understand that different employees have different skills. Don't micromanage—allow employees to use their natural creativity to solve challenges. Identify the strengths and weaknesses of each employee and do your best to assign them to projects and jobs that are a great match for their skills.*

*It is important that you as the manager make an effort to understand your employees as people aside from the job. What* are their passions? What are their hobbies? What gets them up in the morning? Your employees aren't robots that show up each day with no memory of their previous life. While the tendency of many managers is to demand that employees stuff their personality into a little box for the working day, that's an approach guaranteed to waste their potential. Instead, come to understand the employees' perspective and allow them to harness their unique abilities to add value to your business.

And if you really want to build loyalty, look for ways to help them improve the quality of their life. Be willing to accommodate personal situations that may arise from time to time, such as sick children or special family affairs. Maybe allow them to work a flexible schedule (don't accommodate excuses and lies, though).

These are just examples. What's important is that you do your best to meet the needs of your employees as well as ask them to meet the needs of the business.

Putting employees in a position to succeed is only the beginning of the management process, however. Some managers are afraid to hurt feelings while other managers simply don't think providing feedback is worth the time it takes. If you don't confront inappropriate behavior or poor performance, you effectively give permission for more of the same in the future.

The reality is that if an employee is going to grow and improve, they need feedback. The absence of feedback from the boss means they'll find it elsewhere in the form of advice from coworkers or in conversation with friends and family. Unfortunately, most of that feedback isn't going to be helpful, so not only will your employees not improve their performance, they may grow in the wrong direction entirely. They may even adopt bad behavior from other coworkers. Don't ask your employees to fly blind—give them the feedback they need to reach their full potential.

*Embrace and live these concepts: Your people aren't robots. Take advantage of their unique abilities. Understand their passions and their challenges. Provide them feedback as they develop. Do this and you'll enjoy a workforce that is creative, talented, and loyal.*

*You have all the tools you need, and it sounds like your employees still have faith in you, but you are going to have to earn back their trust and their loyalty. I have faith that you can do it.*
*Best of Luck,*
*Vern*

I wanted to turn things around, but had I driven my employees too far away? I felt guilty that I had treated everyone badly for the sake of my vision of productivity. I knew I would have to institute a lot of change to earn back their trust and respect, and part of me wondered if whatever I did would be enough. I was amazed how simple it was to lose their trust, and how daunting it now seemed to get back. I knew it would take time.

# Chapter 8
## ON MY OWN

The sheets and pillows had fallen off the bed. I must have tossed and turned something fierce. Despite hearing from Vern, I still couldn't rest easy that night. I knew I would have to speak to my employees and attempt to rebuild their trust. I was mortified by my actions and how easy it was to ruin someone's faith.

Vern had again handed me wise advice, but I doubted it would be enough. Tommy had given his two weeks if things didn't turn around soon. But what could I do? There seemed to be no possible way to regain anyone's trust in that short time.

Stepping outside that morning, I looked up at the cold, gray sky. The air smelled of a coming rain. Darkness shrouded my hour-long drive to the house. I was left to wonder how in the world I would fix the mess I had got myself into.

I had hoped the drive might clear my head and that I might come up with the right things to say to convince them to stick around. Come on, think.

Could I tell them how valuable they were? No, not enough.

Tell them how much I need them? Starting to sound desperate.

Maybe there was some way I could show them how much they matter? But how could I do that?

Lost in thoughts and talking to myself, I nearly missed the dirt road. As I pulled up the path, I saw the three cars. The gang was all here, except me—mentally, that is.

I walked into the building. The special steel supports we used were still exposed and looked like a gray skeleton, reflecting the ominous clouds. I looked around. On the first floor, my employees were laying the wall structures. Carl was here. There were only three other cars; someone must have given him a ride.

"Everyone!" I yelled to get their attention. "Team meeting in five! Finish up what you're doing!" I could see looks of panic and disgust on everyone's faces. My heart sank. What in God's name was I going to say?

The team gathered around. Daniel and David stood cross-armed, starring at the ground. Tommy was looking at me with cold dead eyes. Everett, hmm, Everett seemed interested, but there was also a look of anguish in his eyes. Everyone must have thought I was about to give them another deadline, another task that would be impossible to complete without working ridiculous hours.

I began, "I've gathered you all here today..."

Tommy started tapping his foot impatiently. The twins twiddled their thumbs.

"...so that I can apologize."

Everyone looked up, interested yet perplexed.

"The truth is," I continued, "I've been working everyone so hard to the point that we've all reached our limits. In a stupid attempt to encourage productivity, I have lied to you. I haven't been accepting your feedback or listening to your issues. I have gone against many of the values I have laid out for communication; simply, I thought, for the sake of efficiency. I don't expect you all to accept my apology—I know you'll want to see the changes for yourself—but I hope you accept that I will change and try to return things to normal. Perhaps better than normal! So what do you say?"

The guys and I exchanged tense glances. The silence was eerie. Finally, Daniel broke the stillness. "I do believe you are sincere; but, to be honest, David and I have started searching for other employment."

"Yeah, and I've started working on my carpenter license," Everett added. "I mean I believe you when you say you'll change, but things aren't just going to go back to the way they were."

"But come on guys," I said. "We had a great thing. I ruined it, but I can rectify it." I started to panic as the guys drifted back to their jobs. "Wait a second! Because I've been so impressed with all your work, and since I have lost some of your faith, how about a fifteen percent bonus for each of you, for the next six months!"

The group turned around, astonished. I hoped I wasn't going to regret what I just promised. Tommy was the first to smile, although it seemed he tried to hide it. Everett was the first to speak, "Well, that's nice and all, but I still want to work towards my licensing. This should help pay for things in the meantime."

The twins turned to each other, talking in Romanian. Finally, they turned to me and said, "OK. Everyone likes getting paid more, but it is just as important that you keep your promise."

I knew giving raises was not the best way to keep employees happy. I had read about other, better means, in an email Vern had sent me when I hired my first few employees. What he said only now popped into my head.

*Dear Jack,*

*I hope all is going well. It is good to know that you are starting to develop an effective workforce. I figured I would share with you a few tips I have learned over the years about dealing with employees.*

*Talented, motivated, and engaged employees are invaluable to your business. That should go without saying.*

*Your employees allow you, as the business owner, to achieve both your short-term goals and long-term vision. Your employees handle the day-to-day work that keeps your company running today, and they are a critical part of the systems you are building which will one day allow your business to run on "autopilot."*

*So it is obvious that keeping your employees engaged should be a top priority. (You'll notice I didn't say "happy." The distinction is subtle but important.) Money is important, but what if you can't afford to give your whole team a raise every year?*

*Here's a little secret I have learned over the years that may surprise you: handing out raises isn't the only way to keep your team engaged. In fact, handing out raises isn't even the best way to keep your team engaged!*

*While competitive pay is important, today we are going to focus on even more important, non-monetary, strategies for keeping your employees focused and dedicated to the goals of the company.*

1. *Create a sense of purpose. Study after study has shown that humans will work harder and more effectively when they believe in the cause they are working toward. If your employees feel like just another cog in the wheel, or feel that their work doesn't make any difference in the scheme of things, even a great paycheck isn't going to keep them motivated. On the other hand, if your team believes that they are changing the world, even in a small way, they will be supremely motivated regardless of the size of their check.*

*However, don't forget that you also need to pay competitive wages for the best talent.*

2. *Invest in your employees. Your employees are giving you forty hours or more each week. They are pouring themselves into your business. Besides money, are you investing in their lives? Whether it is by giving them professional advice or simply by teaching them skills that will aid them throughout their careers when you take the time to give back to your team you are sending the message that you do care. Their loyalty will be your reward.*

3. *Empower your employees. More than anything else, as team members, we all want to feel significant. We want to be respected and appreciated. Micromanaging has the opposite effect; it makes employees feel like robots who cannot be trusted to think for themselves. Instead of micromanaging, train your employees to think for themselves and make the right decisions. Give them as much latitude within your systems as you possibly can. Give them the freedom to "own" their jobs and unleash their creativity. This freedom is more valuable over the long run than any raise!*

*Your employees want more from you than simply money—whether they recognize it or not! (And many of them won't.) These strategies will help you keep your workforce motivated and engaged, and they'll become more productive.*

*Now, that is a win-win for everyone.*

*Best of luck,*

*Vern*

Now I was going to learn that ill-conceived raises were a big mistake. Not only had I fallen victim to panic and tried to bribe my employees into staying, but I had also once again forgotten one of Vern's lessons—and it would cost me. Once everyone heard that I was giving out raises, they all expected one. When members of my other construction team heard about it, they wanted one. The office staff wanted one. It didn't matter who it was, they all wanted one. I had been afraid of losing my crew and had panicked. Now I was rewarding them for the wrong reasons.

Sure, they might have deserved something for my having lied and mistreated them, but I couldn't just bribe them to stay. But this was a temporary measure, I thought. Right? I mean, it wouldn't have lasting repercussions, would it? At least, for now, things would settle down, and I could rebuild after my mistake.

Everyone went back to work. I asked for frequent feedback, and the projects were proceeding smoothly. My second team finished their project and my entire staff now focused on the Corro summer home project.

The bonus helped in the short run, but giving them a raise was just a temporary measure and there was no way I could keep giving unnecessary bonuses and remain profitable. I printed out Vern's points on keeping my employees engaged.

The good news is that with my entire carpentry staff working, it wasn't difficult to create a sense of purpose for them. To witness the entire home finally rise up over the water gave many of them hope. For many of my employees, this was the first time they had built an entire house from scratch.

Even though I had temporarily averted disaster and things appeared to be coming together, we still had the pool and upstairs to do, and I had run out of design ideas. This house had stretched my creativity and nearly tapped all my knowledge of carpentry and architecture. I tried to hide my shortcoming from the crew while, in as subtle a manner as possible, elicit ideas from them. For the most part, they didn't come up with anything I hadn't thought of already, but Daniel and David gave me an interesting idea for the pool that bought some time.

Their idea was simple: create a pool that drew water from the lake. The overflow would return to the lake via an infinity edge that created a waterfall. Completing this design would add a few months to the project, but Chris Corro instantly approved it and substantially padded our budget.

But as everyone became focused on laying the groundwork for the new pool, progress slowed on the home itself. Even though I spent hours researching possibilities for the upstairs, I came up empty handed. I finally decided I needed a new pair of eyes, perhaps someone young and fresh—similar to Everett, but with a degree.

There was no way I could afford a fully qualified architect, so I thought about an intern. After contacting a few universities, around a dozen students expressed interest. Eight of them were still working on their bachelor's degrees and had very little work experience. Three others were working on their master's degrees. But one already had his degree in architecture and was going for his MBA. I don't know why, but his application stood out. His name was Alec.

Alec was a young, eager, boyish-faced man in his early twenties. Instead of just quizzing him, I invited him out to the Corro project to test his insight on a practical project.

His application indicated (to me, at least) that he had come from a fairly privileged background and had only worked a few jobs while in school. He had done something for the college along with a lot of community service. On the day of the interview, he pulled up in a Dodge muscle car equipped with a big V-8 that seemed to make the ground itself shake.

I walked over to the car. "Greetings, you must be Alec!"

"Yes, I am," he said as he got out. "I assume you're Jack?"

"That's right. I brought you out here today because of all the candidates you seemed the most insightful."

"I'd like to think I am," he said. "What is it you're looking for me to do?"

"Follow me upstairs." We walked up to the second floor, which at that time was a big empty space with nothing but a few walls. "We need some creative development for this space. We're currently thinking of having a loft and two bedrooms, but I don't know what to do to really make it pop out. That is why you are here."

Alec paused and rubbed his chin. "To be honest, I was hoping you needed help with management. I suppose I have a few ideas I could draw up, and just looking at the place I think there's plenty to work with."

"I'd like you to work on this project," I replied. "Create some designs and we'll see where we go from there."

"All right," he replied. "I still have a few classes in school, but most days I can work. By the way, you never listed the hours you expected."

"Well, this is an internship, and if I recall, your classes are only on Tuesdays and Thursdays. Can you do Monday, Wednesday, and Friday?"

"Works for me," said Alec. "By the way, who was the architect on this project? I might want to pick his brain a little."

"Well, that would be me."

"You? I thought you were just a carpenter?"

I blushed with embarrassment. Here I was, a guy who never made it through school, claiming to be the architect to a guy who did. "Yes, I'm just a carpenter, but I've managed to do some creative things. I did go to school for architecture, but I had to leave because of a family emergency." I thought I saw Alec scoff, but being self-conscious at the time, it might have just been in my head.

"Well, things look pretty good so far," he said, "but I'm sure I can bring something fresh to the table."

"Sounds good. Go ahead and draw up some ideas. We can meet again next Wednesday."

The two of us parted. My cheeks were still flush and warm. Any conversation about my schooling was always difficult for me, and now that I seemed to have reached my creative limits, I wondered if I had lost the spark.

Over the next few days, Alec proved to have some valuable and creative ideas about the second floor. I didn't entirely understand the design, but more or less the loft became a sunroom of sorts, with a glass balcony extending over the pool. Glass sliding doors led into the sun room. *So much glass!* I thought. I pictured his idea in my head; it would make the room feel like nature itself was right there. The mountain over the lake would look like the largest canvas the room could have.

I didn't fully understand the support structure behind it, though. The glass was fairly new-age and, in theory, could withstand a significant beating; it had good reviews and seemed to have no significant defects. But, it would take some effort to learn how to build a room and balcony almost entirely out of glass. I didn't think anyone on our crew had done anything like it before.

I had an issue with the overall weight of the glass, but both Alec and Tommy seemed sure that because we used reinforced steel on most of the building, the glass would hold up.

I gave them the go ahead. The first shipment of glass would arrive in a week.

Over the next week, I caught Alec toying around on his phone a few times. I didn't call him out for it, as he was just waiting for the glass. At first, I thought I might have been able to use his insight on a few other projects, but then I thought, no, this was my dream; why should he change my ideas? Better to just let him goof off until the glass gets here.

Letting Alec get away with this, however, caused other problems. Although no one directly voiced a complaint, every time I walked in while Alec was goofing off I noticed the rest of the staff watching as if to see what I would do. I'm sure they felt I was treating him preferentially. Tommy approached me on the matter.

"Jack, the rest of the guys have been noticing that Alec's been on his phone a lot. Aren't we going to do anything about it?"

"Look," I said, "just let him know not to play in front of the guys. He's just here for the second floor, and we're still a week away from working on that. Remind everyone he's just an intern. He is not getting paid very much, and besides, he is here for a specific job."

"And what job is that?" said Tommy. "He barely talks to anyone except you. I mean, he consulted with me briefly on the support structures, and he was very easy to work with, but he's here almost seven hours a day, and he hasn't done a thing otherwise. It's even getting to me. Look, I understand that you want an expert to help out. I get it. But we can't just let him goof off; it really damages morale."

I wanted to explode. *Who is Tommy to think that I need anyone, expert or no expert, to get the job done?* I contained myself. His feedback was important after all—at least, that is what my company beliefs stated, right? I responded, "Look, just make sure he's not screwing around in front of the other guys. Once the glass gets here, make sure he gets that job done." My phone rang. "Tommy, I have to take this. It looks like it's Lisa, so it must be important. I think Alec is invaluable and if his behavior is disrupting things, find a way around it."

"Fine, I'll deal with it, as usual." He walked away.

"Hello Lisa, what's up?" I said.

"Hey Jack, listen, I've just done the books for the month and well..." She paused. I heard a long sigh through the phone.

"Well, what is it?"

"Umm, well it seems as though we're barely going to break even this quarter. I mean, Chris has substantially padded our budget, but with our current line of development and the bonus you handed out, Jack's will barely make any money as a company."

"Oh—" Another word came to mind following that, which I would never utter. "What's our bottom line here?"

"Well, for one, we need another job. We have two teams working on one project, and—I need to emphasize this—based on the numbers, we should have two projects going. We are well ahead of schedule on the Corro home, and I think it would be best if we move the second team to something simpler that will bring in quick revenue, like a kitchen refurbishment or something. Otherwise, based on the way things are going, we won't be able to keep up."

"Fine, fine," I said. "Start searching for a new project for one of the teams, something easy, just a month or two of work. I want to get Corro's house done. He has offered us several million dollars, and at the end of the day that will balance the budget!"

"OK, Jack, I'll see what I can come up with, but I haven't heard from anyone in months, and it seems like the market may be dry. I can't guarantee any jobs will come our way."

I knew our marketing was minimal. I was always counting on the big jobs. Erica always warned about having "all our eggs in one basket," but that seemed too cliché to take seriously. Besides, I wasn't sure we needed the additional jobs. I thought this job, the Corro house, would put our name out there in a powerful way. I was still obsessed with the current project; if it was done right, I thought, we might not even need marketing—our jobs would be our marketing! Everything seemed like it would work out all right.

When the first of the glass arrived, I just stared at it. The massive crystal formed a half arc rising out of the truck. The thing was almost four inches thick and had been custom-designed to allow for another custom-built glass sliding door to be built into the wall, sliding through a one-inch cut in the glass. I still wasn't sure about the details of this new age glass; all I knew was that it was some chemical compound that allowed extra durability and made it very easy to shape. Alec described that it was made using a process similar to the making of Plexiglas. However it was made, I couldn't help but say out loud, and "Couldn't hail chip this stuff? Or any severe weather or falling branches?"

Alec must have overheard me. Out of the corner of my eye, I saw him bend over and pick something up. I turned and saw a rock the size of his fist fly out of his hand straight at the glass pane. Everything suddenly went into slow motion. Tommy jumped up and ran to intercept it. I just stood there gawking. What the heck was Alec thinking? Those panes cost over a hundred thousand dollars!

The rock hit its mark and bounced harmlessly off.

See?" Alec shouted. "Nothing to worry about. The thing is as tough as bulletproof glass."

*That was wildly unacceptable!* I walked over to the glass. If there had been any damage, I would have fired him on the spot. I looked at the impact mark. There was a bit of rock dust that I easily wiped off with the tip of my finger. The surface of the glass was still smooth and pristine.

Tommy went over to Alec and started in on him, "What the hell were you thinking? Imagine if that thing shattered! Imagine the cost! Imagine the time it would take to get a new one made! I mean seriously. We can read the specs. There was no reason to hurl a rock at it!"

Alec seemed oblivious. "Chill. No harm, no foul."

Tommy was red with anger.

I came over. "Hey guys, relax. Nothing went wrong. Alec, next time, please don't chuck rocks at anything—period."

Tommy grabbed me by the arm. "Can I talk to you for a minute?"

We went behind the building, where Tommy said, "That kind of behavior is completely intolerable, and you know it. He should be fired! And if that incident wasn't bad enough, he has played on his phone most of the time he has been here. The guys all feel he looks down on them just because they never went to college."

"OK, OK—I hear you," I said. I was worried that if I fired Alec when he hadn't caused any real damage, the other guys would think I was just being nasty to him. I tried to reassure Tommy, "Tommy, you are right about his behavior. I think we need to keep a better eye on him. But we need him right now. He does good work when he's working, and his idea for the second floor was brilliant. Let's just keep tabs on him. Besides, now that the glass is here, he'll be kept busy. Let's just see how things work out."

Alec and Tommy successfully installed the first pane within only a day. Alec was finally working in a way that didn't bother the rest of the crew. That day was bright and sunny, and everything seemed all right with the world. With Alec doing the creative thinking, Lisa doing the books, and Tommy handling the crews, I thought that maybe I could take a long-deserved rest for a few days. After all, things were going smoothly, and it seemed like my ideas, and creative input wouldn't be missed. I didn't know whether to be happy or upset about the situation—could I be so easily replaced? But, because I wanted everything to work for me autonomously someday, it seemed like a good time to take a break.

Before heading to my car, I did a quick round through the building. I could swear I saw Everett slip his cell phone into his pocket when I walked by him. I got in the car. For the first time, I was leaving for home before five. Everything will be OK; I said to myself. The drive home was lovely; the sun shone through the trees and reflected green waves of light. Everything seemed to glow.

As I arrived home, I noticed a silver Jeep parked along the curb between my house and the neighbor's house. Getting out of the car, I looked up at the sun again to let its warmth sooth my face. I stood there in the silence for a few moments.

I entered the house, wondering where Erica might be. I heard some faint chattering coming from the living room, and then I noticed a familiar overcoat and hat hung on the rack. Vern was here! I felt my heart leap. I always enjoyed his company. What a perfect end to a near-perfect day!

I hurried through the hall, eager to greet both my friend and my wife, but as I rounded the corner into the living room, my heart instantly sunk. Erica had a somber look and seemed almost on the verge of tears. Vern was facing away.

He turned around. "Jack, it's good to see you."

"Hi, Vern. You, too. It's been a while, welcome to our home. I see you've met Erica. So what brings you to our part of town?"

"Well, Jack, I wasn't sure when I'd see you again. I figured I'd stop by and see how you were and how things were going."

"Is there something wrong?"

"Alan—my youngest son—and his wife are expecting their first baby. In fact, they're having twins! They're going to need a lot of help, so my wife and I are going to Argentina to be with them. I don't know when we will be able to return, but it won't be for many months. This will be our last meeting for quite a while, so please bring me up to speed on where you are now."

# Chapter 9
## THE BASICS

ongratulations to your son and his wife," I said. "You must be thrilled. How's my business? A tad slow, to be honest. I have only got one major project going—the Chris Corro house—and we might need to look for another job. But the payout on the Corro house is pretty massive, plus it will be like free marketing at the end of the day."

Vern let out a long sigh. "Well, things don't sound too bad. And by Chris Corro you mean the country singer, right?"

I nodded.

"Well, that's great. And yes, it will give you free marketing, and will help for sure, but you can't just use your famous jobs to land you new ones. What's your current marketing strategy?"

*Marketing strategy?* I had heard the term but never really thought about it. I always thought my work spoke for itself, and that seemed to be the way things were working. "Well, we've got a website, and Lisa has been searching for new leads."

"But what's your *strategy*?"

"Well, we're trying to—"

Vern cut me off. "I take it you don't really know what marketing strategy means, do you?"

"Well, no. Not really."

"That's OK. Most people don't. I know you have been relying on referrals, which is not bad, but you need a new job, and you have got to hunt for it. Correct?" I nodded. "So what I tell all my marketers and fellow CEO's is: message, market, and match."

"Umm… OK."

"You look baffled," said Vern. "Let's start with the *message*. You know what you are selling, don't you?"

"Sure. We want to bring innovative solutions to construction and architectural strategies to better improve a building's utility, whether that be creating multipurpose rooms or bringing new design elements that improve ascetics or effectiveness."

"Excellent! You've got your product down. Now you have to bring in new customers, advertise what you want to be known for (your product/ your brand), have satisfied customers recommend you to friends and family, and bring to bear the message you just laid out.

"Now let's talk about the *market*," he continued. "You have to get your message out there working for you, and, based on your history, your strength has been good recommendations. People love your work and are advocating for you. Right? All you have to do is find the right customers who fit what you do—not only customers who want your product but customers with whom *you* want to work."

"What customers do I want?" I asked. "Don't I want every customer? I mean, at the end of the day, it's all about profit, isn't it?"

"Well, yes and no. A bad customer can harm you. As the saying goes, 'never wrestle with a pig: he'll enjoy it immensely and you won't.' Occasionally, some customers will simply whine and complain—I don't like this, I don't like that, you are taking too long, when will this get done, I don't like the way it looks, feels, tastes, smells, sounds—whether or not any of that really matters to them. These customers will drag you down. Bear in mind, I'm assuming you are doing everything in your power to please them, but some people simply cannot be pleased."

"Aren't you over generalizing, Vern?" I said. "Some people might just be speaking their minds."

"Some people, yes. But if you know you have done everything you could, and they are still pointing out minutia, they might not be the customer for you. When you are targeting a high-end client, there are bound to be some who are very demanding.

"So, before you start working with them, make sure you can deliver on your message to them. And understand that for a few, it might be impossible."

"OK," I said. "Let's see if I understand you. Some customers I want because they're truly looking for my specific product. I have to know I can deliver that product to them. Otherwise, they could spoil everything with a bad review. But how do I find the right customer who fits with what I offer?"

"That is the *match*," he replied. "That means you find the overlap of the customer who wants what you offer and that is something you can deliver. You have to, in a way, interview your customers. You want to make sure that their expectations and your product line up."

"Based on that," I said, "I take it online marketing wouldn't be the appropriate way to get the right customers."

"It helps put your name out there," said Vern. "Also, a professionally done website will help explain what you are about, show off some of your previous jobs, and demonstrate positive customer reviews."

"These days, a website seems like the only way to get a name out there," I said. "Isn't that the best way to attract people to my product?"

Vern looked up with a slight smirk. "Ah, but that is just one of the marketing elements. You have a product, and you are trying to find someone who wants it. But there is a second element to marketing many people seem to forget about: you know there are people out there who want something you provide, so you have to find a way to *sell* to them. For example, someone is probably out there looking to build a unique, high-end home who might be interested in your special design—but that person doesn't know that you exist or even that what you are offering is possible.

"Jack, I remember you telling me about your first job, back when you were just a contractor and not an entrepreneur. You worked for a realty group. Perhaps they know someone who has a luxury home project, whereas the guys you worked with on the hotel might not have the kind of project you are looking for because they only do large-scale commercial projects."

"They have already been in contact with us," I said. "They had a big project at one of their other hotels that we had to turn down because we couldn't bring the necessary manpower."

"Exactly," said Vern. "Another person you could ask is Chris Corro."

"But we haven't even finished his home yet."

"But he likes the work you are doing, correct? And he's local, on top of that."

"I guess," I replied.

"Maybe you could give him a call. He knows what you are all about and might have some friends in the area who are planning homes."

"I could do that," I said.

"Just keep in mind the basics of marketing when searching for new clients. Do your research. Identify your market. Learn the needs and thoughts of your customers; find a way to reach out, communicate with them, and attempt to create lines of communication. Get them interested in what you have to offer and what makes you unique, and if they don't know what you are all about, let them know! Once you have created a dialogue, keep learning what your customers want and how you can fulfill their needs. Keep the lines of communication and the dialogue going until you finally land the sale. And it doesn't stop there!"

"What?" I asked. "Once I have the sale isn't the marketing done? I assume I still need to communicate about the job and the details of getting it done, but isn't marketing over at that point?"

"Oh heavens no, Jack! As I said before, your customers can often be your best resource for future marketing. How many times have you told someone about an amazing product you bought and they went and bought one as well?"

I guess I looked like I wasn't entirely getting his point because Vern sighed again and looked up at the ceiling as if in thought. "Well, let me think of a good example. Ah! Think of Apple computers. They aren't going to be the cheapest. If people just wanted a machine with lots of features at a low price, there are plenty of alternatives. What Apple offers is a great design, flawless performance, and excellent customer service."

"But isn't customer service part of the product they offer?"

"Precisely! But it is also a marketing tool. Let's say you and your friend have two different machines—you bought a Dell, and he built his own. Both of your computers break at the same time. While he has to spend many hours trying to fix it, maybe even involving a lot of research to figure out what the problem is, all you have to do is give Dell a call and within a few hours your computer is up and running again. You then tell your friend, "You should have gotten a Dell," and suddenly you just became an extension of Dell marketing. In the future, your friend might just get a Dell computer."

"I think I understand. So in keeping the lines of communication open, I would be keeping my business in the minds of my customer so they will spread the word."

"Exactly!" said Vern. "If you want to get your product out there, try keeping in touch with your previous customers. Let them know what new thing you are doing. You can accomplish this with something as simple as an occasional email or phone call. Just keep in touch!"

I was becoming excited by our conversation and couldn't wait to use Vern's suggestions to help bail me out of the company's present situation. Enthusiastic, I said, "All right, that solves one problem!"

Vern tilted his head and squinted at me, "What do you mean? I thought you said things were going well, minus the marketing issue."

"Well, sort of," I stuttered. "But it is not that big of a deal."

"Come on, now, Jack. Don't be coy with me. Nothing you can say to this old man will give him a heart attack."

Shoot. I was caught. I started, "Well, I'm just having a bit of trouble with a grad student we recently hired..."

"Ha! Yeah, sometimes those fresh out of college kids can be . . . well . . . fresh. What's he doing?"

"He has only been doing real work since we got these new glass panes we're installing. Before that, he was goofing around on his phone. But when the glass first arrived he showed off to make a point by hurling a rock at the stuff."

"Say what? Did it break?"

"No, no. The glass is virtually unbreakable. But it was unacceptable and reckless behavior!" I thought I knew what Vern was going to say: Fire the kid, or scold him, or something like that.

"Did you tell him on day one what acceptable behavior is?" asked Vern.

"Hmmm? Isn't proper behavior implied?"

"Heh, heh," he chuckled. "Well, recent grads bring their own challenges to the table. For one, don't assume that anything goes without saying. One of the big liabilities of recent graduates is that they often have no experience in the world of business. So from dress code to protocol while dealing with other employees and clients, you have to make sure that your new employee understands your expectations. What was his name again?"

"Alec."

"So next time you see Alec or hire any inexperienced employee, lay out all the rules of etiquette and proper behavior. Has Alec been doing any technical work?"

"Sort of," I replied. "He and Tommy have been installing the glass together. I don't think Alec has the technical skills necessary to do it himself."

"Good. You must recognize that any new hire is like a blank canvas; you must teach that person everything from scratch. Now is your chance to teach him how to do everything your way. Take the time to show your new employee how everything is done in your company. If you fail to teach a given process, it will be up to the employee to figure out how to get it done—and you may not be happy with the results. Alec, for instance, is on his phone because he doesn't know anything except the big projects you assign him. Teach him to do some simple dirty work while he has some down time.

"One other thing to keep in mind: career expectations have changed. Nowadays, few college graduates expect to spend their career working for a single business. You will have to work harder to keep your talented employees engaged and happy. The best way to do this is to encourage open dialogue. You shouldn't hesitate to point out areas in need of improvement, and your employees should be able to express frustrations or other issues."

"Even if I can bring Alec up a notch and make him more efficient," I responded, "that doesn't handle what's really been bothering me." I let out a long breath. I had yet to say this to anyone, but I forged ahead: "I feel like I have lost the spark, Vern. It just seems like with Alec doing the creative thinking, Tommy managing perfectly fine, and everyone else seeming to be just fine as well; I don't feel needed."

Vern looked me over before asking, "Are you excited to go to work every day?

"No," I replied.

"Are your employees?"

"I don't know. But I don't think 'excited' would be the right word."

"Then why do you do what you do?" he asked.

"It's what I've always done, I suppose."

"So you are not passionate about what you do anymore?"

"It's not that," I replied. "It just feels like I'm only going through the motions at this point, and I think that might go for my staff as well."

"That makes sense—and it happens often. You see, as a business grows, and things maybe become routine, it can be easy for that spark to fade. But if you find a way to bring that spark back to life, you'll be able to work more effectively, and you'll have more fun doing it. I have a few simple ideas that might help.

"For one, operate on principles, not on rules. While some very specific directions need to be formalized, creating an excessive amount of regulations, rules, and inflexible policies only forces employees to follow the letter of the law and ignore the principles that really matter. The best way to empower your employees is to give them creative leeway. Let them solve problems and take advantage of opportunities. Don't script every step they take; instead, let them achieve the results. You don't have many rules you enforce, so cultivating principles from what you believe should be relatively simple."

"So for instance," I asked, "when I lay out proper etiquette to Alec, I shouldn't tell him everything he is not supposed to do? Rather, I should lay out what are the principles of good work etiquette, such as proving that a pane of glass is durable by referring to the specs rather than throwing a rock at it?"

"Something like that," said Vern. "Also, instead of telling him not to goof off when he has down time, let him know what he should be doing, like assisting others."

"OK. I think I understand. Don't try to over-manage with rules, and let my employees work things out according to the company's principles. What's next?"

"Let's see," said Vern as he rubbed his chin. "Usually, I tell my managers to keep the paperwork where it belongs. Don't bog your employees down in paperwork unless that is the focus of their job. Forcing your managers and crew to battle piles of paperwork is one of the quickest ways to burn them out. Let them solve problems and do their jobs—don't make them fill out forms and reports that don't add value."

"You mean like how I continually ask Tommy for status updates when I'm not there? And how I continually ask my staff about the details of their work?"

"That's not exactly paperwork. You could call it 'verbal paperwork' though, couldn't you? So yes, asking about every detail of what your staff and crew are doing just bogs them down and doesn't add value. They'll lose their passion. Then again, you do still need to keep informed so that you know which staff are succeeding and which are not."

"And if I know that, then what?" I asked.

"Well, if they're not succeeding you might need to find a new way to encourage them. Sometimes you might want to find out what's going on in their personal lives; for all you know, they may be having troubles at home that are disrupting their work. If necessary, you might need to let them go." He took a deep breath before continuing. "On the other hand, acknowledge high achievers. If you acknowledge and reward the efforts of your best workers, you are sending the message that performance counts. Whether it is a promotion, a raise, a bonus, or an award, provide some incentive for each of your high achievers."

"Tommy has been doing exceptional work, and so have the twins. Maybe I should give them a raise? But what do you mean by an 'award'?"

"That could be any number of things," said Vern. "A gift certificate for a family dinner is a nice example."

"Thanks, Vern. That gives me a few ideas on how to reinvigorate my staff, but it doesn't touch my personal dilemma of feeling uninspired and not needed."

"Do you spend some time on a regular basis brainstorming new ideas?"

"Yes. I do a bit of research every week about new construction techniques, materials, and ideas."

"So you are just doing research on your products?"

"Yeah. What else is there?"

"Ha! No wonder you feel like your tank's run dry! You are looking for new ideas and creating new ideas in the wrong place!"

"What? How is that?" Vern's comment startled me.

"Well, Jack, take a moment to think about it: as a business owner and entrepreneur, your job is to innovate, correct?"

I nodded. It seemed like a simple concept.

"So that doesn't just mean innovating your product—you now have Alec to do that, but looking for innovation in other areas as well, like changing your marketing strategy, expanding your operation, hiring more teams, and finding ways to bring in more top-notch employees. Remember, you are not just a product innovator, you are a business innovator!"

Vern was pushing me beyond my simple ideas of what being in business for myself was about. "Seems doable," I said. "It certainly seems a much more effective way to invigorate myself and my employees than I have done in the past."

"Oh, do tell," he seemed to chide. "And what did you do?"

I didn't want to answer, but I now had *honesty is the best policy* seared into my mind. I had to let him in on my dark secret. "You may recall, Vern, a few months back I was working the crew too hard and not listening to their feedback."

"A fairly common mistake, especially when you get over involved with the job. I assume it was that Corro job."

"Yes. And I just wanted to increase efficiency. I wanted the job done so badly and done right that I pushed their limits."

"Nothing wrong with pushing limits as long as you remember that people can burn out."

"Well, they did—all of them. And they all were looking for other employment."

"That's only natural; sometimes people reach a tipping point. And business owners more often than not will push employees, frequently thinking they are just robots—"

"But I did more than that," I interrupted. "I treated them like animals! Like slaves! I almost couldn't live with myself. I was in the wrong! I went against everything you taught me. I didn't know what to do."

"Hold on, Jack. Calm down. Everyone makes mistakes. You are still in business right? So you must have settled it. I'm interested in how you managed that."

I gulped so loudly that he must have heard it. I had done the opposite of what he once told me. How on earth would I explain it? Telling the truth is often more painful than a lie, but I couldn't lie. He had to know.

My mind raced. I couldn't believe what I was thinking; my business, my entire life revolved around Vern. I was about to lose him. What was I going to do? Every action I seemed to take led me deeper and deeper into the abyss, and ignoring Vern's advice—was that now my habit? Over and over he had told me how to work with employees, how to keep them happy, but I went against him, and now I had to face the music. I began, "Listen, I—"

"Come on, Jack. Out with it."

"When all my employees were looking for other employment, I panicked and gave them all a six-month bonus."

"You did what?" Vern said, astonished.

"I thought they deserved a bonus. I had been wrong to treat them like I did and to work them like mules."

"No! Sure you were wrong. But a six-month bonus? You are barely breaking even!" He was emphatic.

"I know—but I couldn't lose my employees and I didn't know what else to do. I apologized and gave them a bonus because I didn't think I could change things fast enough to convince them to stay."

"There were plenty of other ways you could apologize to them, but when you give bonuses for no valid reason, it poisons your company. I mean, how many of your other staff approached you and said, 'Hey, we deserve a bonus too!' even though you hadn't mistreated them?"

"Pretty much everyone," I said.

"Exactly. That is one expensive lesson, isn't it? And the next time you or your manager Tommy does something wrong, won't they be expecting a raise? So now, instead of trying to earn a raise by working hard and doing their best, they'll just be waiting for someone higher up to screw up and have to apologize."

"But I can still turn things around, can't I? All I need to do is encourage them, give them feedback and purpose, right?"

"Paradoxically, it's simple—at least when you sound it out," said Vern. "But turning around company culture never happens overnight. Let me ask you, before you gave everyone a raise, before you worked them hard, did you look at your three-year plan? Were you acting according to your objectives, or were you just reacting impulsively?"

He had me here. I hadn't considered my three-year plan. I hadn't even written it out. I had only written out a few weeks of a plan then got so caught up with work that I forgot to revisit my goals. I had hardly even laid out any short-term plans. "Impulsively," I stuttered. "I haven't—well, I haven't been keeping up with my plans."

Vern heaved a long sigh before saying, "That was the very first lesson I taught you: planning. Have you even been listening? If you sat down and planned, if you had calculated your actions before you acted, would you be in this situation of barely scraping by? Your business isn't even close to where you want it to be! I understand it is difficult to follow through on everything, but planning is the most important thing you can do as a business owner.

"How can you fulfill your dream, bring your business to fruition without planning? I know you are capable of it, but even if I coach you all day long, if you don't use even my most basic advice, you'll just struggle at the bottom." Vern glanced at his watch. "Jack, I need to be going. You'll do just fine if you remember our discussions and reflect on them as you make your daily plans and decisions."

As I heard these words it seemed to me that he was saying, "Jack, my businesses will do fine without me—will yours?"

We said our goodbyes before going outside. I watched as his taillights vanished in the darkness.

Erica stood next to me. Her warm smile faded when she saw look on my face. Perhaps sensing that I wasn't in the mood to talk, she went in the house while I sat on the front step.

I felt a vibration in my pocket. It was Tommy calling me. I ignored it. I would check voice mail or look for a text message later. A few seconds later the phone started vibrating again. Still Tommy. *Just leave me a message!* I was tempted to lob my phone as far as I could.

Tommy called a third time. I answered.

"Jack," he said, panting loudly into the phone. "Jack, thank God I was able to reach you. Something happened."

I tried to calm him down. "Easy, Tommy. OK, tell me what happened."

"Well, I left my wallet at the Corro house and had to drive back to get it. And, when I got there, well . . ." he stopped to catch his breath.

"Tommy, what the heck is going on?"

"The house, Jack. The house has collapsed!"

# Chapter 10
# FALLOUT

D read—that's all I felt. And horror. I wanted to break down then and there. Desperately holding onto my composure, I asked, "What do you mean, 'It collapsed'?"

"Well, not the entire thing, just the back end. Oh, shoot! I've got to run! Can you get up here ASAP?"

"I'll be there as soon as I can." I ran into the house. "Erica!" I yelled, "I've got to head off. There's an emergency at the Corro house!" I bolted out the door.

I sped my way through the winding New Hampshire roads. I tried calling Tommy a few times to get more detail, but no answer. I couldn't help but imagine the house looking like a pile of rubble. Even if it wasn't that bad, Tommy was still in a panic. I figured it couldn't be anything short of a disaster—a disaster I couldn't afford. I hoped I was lucky, and the cause was something insurance would cover!

My headlights swept across the towering house as I pulled up on the dirt road. The walls, the roof—still intact! The only oddity was two lonely taillights from Tommy's truck peeping out from behind the home. I pulled in and went over to the truck. Scanning the house as I walked around, everything still seemed fine, until I saw why Tommy's truck was where it was. A thick, heavy rope led from its front end into the lake. The truck's headlights revealed the mud-covered surface of an entire wall. Looking a little closer, I noticed a curved shape—that distinctive curve.

I looked around. The back end of the house had completely fallen and slid away, creating a trail littered with scraps of concrete, steel, and plaster on the slope between the house and lake. It looked like over half of the back of the house was strewn across the landscape.

I saw Tommy, and walked over and sat down next to him.

"So," I began, calmly, "do you mind telling me what in the hay is going on here?" I noticed his pants were wet and covered in mud.

After letting out a long groan, he began his explanation. "I left today around five thirty. Everyone else was long gone. Before I left, though, I double-checked to make sure the glass panel was properly installed. Everything looked fine. On my way home, my stomach started growling, so I stopped at a fast food joint for a burger. It was there I noticed my wallet was missing, so much for my snack. Now, I ended up having to haul back here. I wandered in thinking everything was fine and dandy, but then I stepped through the front door and what did I find?"

I knew his question was rhetorical, but I went ahead and asked, "What?"

"Like you see now: the entire back end of this house was gone. Literally, just gone. Of course, I freaked out! I looked first for that big pane of glass. Because I didn't see any shards strewn across the hill, I was hopeful that the honking expensive piece might have survived. So I followed the trail of debris and didn't find it. But something that big doesn't just disappear! I finally got the idea to go into the water. Don't ask me why, but I did it."

At this point, the anticipation was killing me. "And?"

"As I was wading in, my foot hit a solid surface. I felt around in the muck. Miraculously the entire panel survived!"

"Thank the good Lord above!" I said. "Alec told us that stuff was tough."

"Yeah. Thank God. Anyways, I pulled up the truck, ran some rope from the truck to the panel, and tried to pull it out of the water. As you saw, I only got it out part of the way. I didn't have enough traction under the tires to pull the entire thing out, but at least, it won't sink." He let out a long sigh.

"Hey, Tommy, you did fine," I said. "I'm very glad to have you, and I'm grateful you were here to help with this."

"I'm glad you came as well. After calling you twice, I was worried you might not answer. There's no way I could get the rest of this thing out of that mud by myself. Anyway, since I knew it'd take you a while to get here, I did a bit of snooping around."

"Yeah? And what did you find?"

"Well, I'm no engineer, but it looks like one of the support beams collapsed. I'm not sure why it did, but if I were a betting man, I would say it was one of two things."

"Was the support defective—or did we install it wrong?"

"I checked it out. The beam didn't break, fully. And the installation looked fine—on the surface." He paused for a moment, seeming deep in thought. I wondered if he was thinking the same as I: Did we install it incorrectly? Did I drive my employees to the point where they rushed and made a mistake? Did they forget to examine the beam and check for cracks? Something *did* go wrong, and all I could think about was what I may have done to cause it.

It actually didn't matter what the physical cause was because ultimately I was to blame.

Tommy continued, "Anyway, the only explanation I could come up with is that the support must have been weak already, which is why it buckled. However, the supports next to it should have held the weight. By the looks of it, when the first one collapsed its neighbors were pushed out of place."

"Do you know who installed the other supports?" I asked.

"I'm pretty sure we all had a part to play, except Everett. I know you, and I worked on one of the supports and the twins on the others. I think we just missed something in the process."

It was clear that nobody was to blame for this mess but myself. "Well," I said, feeling miserable but choosing to stay positive, "at least no one got hurt. Let's pull this glass out of the mud and then I'll take you to dinner."

Smiling appreciatively, he said, "All right, let's get to it."

We spent an hour hauling the massive panel onto shore and tying it down. By the time we were finished we were both wet, muddy, and tired as all-get-out. On the way home we stopped at a fast food restaurant. It was the only place open nearby, and was probably the only place that didn't care how filthy we were! I didn't get home before 11:30 that night; I'm sure Tommy didn't either. Lucky him, though—he had tomorrow off.

The next morning I woke up late. No one was going to be on site, but I had to go and clean up after the disaster. I figured I would go in late and first take some time to write out my yearlong goals and projections. This morning everything seemed pretty bleak; repairing the damage would easily cost $100,000 out of my pocket. The only upside to the disaster was that the glass survived; otherwise, I would be out far more, and it would be impossible to fix.

Erica tried to comfort me by telling me that I was successful and was working a good job. Her comment irritated me, even though she was right—at least partially. I wanted desperately to be an entrepreneur, but I never planned for what that entailed. Even though I might be able to take a day off now and then, I was basically just working a glorified job, only with me as my own boss and me as my own employee. And unlike my old paycheck job, if I disappeared for even just a little while things, could go horribly wrong.

My three-year goal was more daunting than ever. At first, it had seemed like a challenge, except now I felt like I had taken several steps back. I figured I had better take a more concrete approach and turn my overall three-year goal into three separate one-year goals, each broken into quarterly goals. For now, the plan was to rebuild. While I couldn't take the time to look for other jobs and still finish the Corro house in time, I asked Lisa to talk to our previous clients and to poke our nose around out there.

There was no question planning was important, but right now it also seemed to me keeping positive was just as important, if not more so.

How could I do this? I asked myself.

Then I gave myself the answer: "Vern would know."

I know this may sound silly, but I decided to write myself an email—Vern's "response" to my "How to stay positive" question. Here's what I wrote to myself:

*Dear Jack,*

*As much as I would like to avoid them, setbacks are part of every business operation.*

*Setbacks affect the smallest corporations and largest businesses—but they carry an extra element of danger for small businesses. That's because most small businesses are dependent on the energy and focus of a single owner—you. In addition to whatever the direct consequences of a setback are, the possibility that the owner could give in to negativity and lose his drive and determination is fatal to the business. How you respond to failure and negativity will determine the ultimate success or failure of your venture.*

*How can you stay positive in the midst of failure?*

*Consider your influences. Make sure you have positive, inspiring individuals to rely on. You may not need them most of the time, but when setbacks happen, having strong positive influences can mean the difference between getting back on your feet or staying down for the count.*

*Prepare yourself in advance. At some point in the future, you'll experience failure, setbacks, or seemingly impossible challenges. Setbacks are part of every business—they are simply stepping-stones on the path to success. Expect them, and you'll be able to keep them in perspective when they occur.*

*Don't get carried away when things are good. As every sports figure or politician can tell you, getting too high when things are good only leads to crushing disappointment when things go bad. Keep as even a keel as possible—remember that good times are rarely as good as they seem, and bad times rarely as bad. It may be hard to control how down you feel when things do go wrong, but by keeping focused and realistic during the good times, you can avoid dramatic emotional swings.*

*Stay focused on your goal. When you approach problems from a big-picture perspective, you will realize that setbacks are just part of the journey. By keeping focused on your goals, the inevitable challenges will not seem nearly so overwhelming.*

*Note: Don't skim through this section and say "I'm doing great, this doesn't apply to me." It does apply to you.*
*Yours, Jack*

I couldn't believe I wrote that to myself. It seemed crazy. But who cared? It worked for me. Although in the face of this overwhelming failure, how could I possibly see this in a positive light? I looked back through my notes and found Vern's advice on viewing failure as progress. It gave me hope, not just that this setback could lead to progress, but that a piece of Vern would always be with me. So now I had to take the lessons he had taught me, and maybe—just maybe—I could turn things around.

Vern's advice about company culture stood out to me. But that doesn't just change overnight, he always said. When he had first mentioned "company culture," I immediately pictured some tenured professor rambling on and on from some ivory tower, far away from the "real world" of business. And while academia has certainly created its fair share of theories that look great on paper but don't work in real life, company culture isn't one of them, he had assured me. A strong company culture is extremely valuable to a business.

He once asked me if I had ever visited an Apple store. I had, so I knew exactly what a strong company culture looked like. Apple does a great job of incorporating their employees into their culture, and the vast majority of employees truly buy in. Ask a customer associate to tell you about their latest laptop, for instance, and you'll see an authentic passion and sincerity as he or she answers that no amount of sales training can produce—it cannot be faked. From the ground up, Apple employees buy into Apple's culture. And doesn't Apple's continuing success speak for itself?

A strong company culture is about much more than sales. In fact, the productivity of your workforce is greatly impacted by the power of your culture. Here's an analogy. Have you ever seen a professional sports team that just doesn't care, that has totally quit on their coach? They're still out there playing (after all, they want to get paid!), but they aren't doing the little things right, and they aren't pulling together. Contrast that with a team that buys into the program their coach has created. They hustle. They dive on every loose ball. They finish every play. They sink or swim as a team. The difference? The first team doesn't buy into their organizational culture; the second team does. What kind of team did I want? The second, of course!

I asked myself what I should do.

First, I had to define my culture: What did I stand for? What were my company values? What was I passionate about?

Second, I would need to introduce my culture to my employees— and I would need them to buy in. I knew this was easier said than done. It would take repetition, training, positive reinforcement, and most importantly, it would take me practicing what I preached. I was the boss—I set the tone. If I wasn't living up to the standards and the values I had identified, nobody else would.

The strength of my company culture would be more important than the quality of each of my products. It would be more important than my profit margin. It would be more important than any marketing campaign. If I could get my culture right, everything else would follow. A company with a strong culture would produce quality products, naturally enjoy a healthy profit margin, and generate word-of-mouth advertising. Culture beats strategy any day.

Looking at my plan, I realized that my biggest issue was the culture I had already established. Did this mean I had to ignore my plan and just work on the culture for the short term? No, but I did have to have a plan to straighten out my company culture. Whereas I had always assumed company culture was simply a communication issue, communication is really just part of the broader picture.

Things weren't all bad, so I wondered what I had actually done right. It seemed like one of them was keeping positive in the face of a disaster; even Tommy seemed happier once I showed up and appeared to be in a semi-good mood (despite the way I truly felt). So part of my company culture would be to keep positive even when the news was negative, and to view setbacks as a means to progress.

OK. That's good. Now, what was causing problems? Well, Alec goofing off while at work was certainly an issue—but how could I address it without isolating or alienating him? That's simple: work is for work. If your task is finished, help out others or communicate with a manager about other tasks. And when you are on break, take it out of the work environment. This is what I always did, so it seemed fair to expect it from everyone else.

I kept working in this fashion until I discovered a formula for creating my company culture. I wrote it down in the same way Vern gave me notes. Now I was making my own.

What type of company culture did my organization need? The answer depended upon the objective of my business and the expectations I had of my employees.

Here are the primary questions to pinpoint the culture:

- Will employees work primarily in teams, or individually?
- Is competition among my employees or teams desirable?
- Is a rigid management structure necessary?
- Will some or all of my employees regularly interact with customers?
- How large is my business currently, and how much do I expect to grow?
- Which values are important to my organization? Examples include honesty, a tireless work ethic, good humor, and selflessness.
- What type of workplace environment do I want to create? Will it be fun, relaxed, highly professional, and fast-paced?

As I answered these questions, it became very easy to identify the traits of the culture I wanted to create. I wanted a team-oriented, non-competitive environment, with a focus on getting the job done to near-perfect quality. I wanted to keep the environment relaxed enough for individual growth while ensuring that team projects ran like clockwork.

Now that I had laid out the foundation for my culture, I had to make a plan—a doable three-month plan—to implement it and bring my employees on board. I wrote down how I would succeed in doing this. There was no way around it: the effort would demand major commitment and leadership on my part.

First things first.

1. Bring my management team on board.

Before presenting the guidelines for my new culture to my employees, it would be essential that my management team be fully on board. This meant both Tommy and Lisa. They would play a crucial role in the implementation of my culture, both by setting an example and by ensuring employee buy-in. It would be essential that I didn't proceed until my managers were on the same page as me, as confusion at this level would sabotage the entire process.

2. Explain new expectations, as well as benefits, to my teams.

If I expected changes from my employees, I would have to explain my new expectations thoroughly while explaining how these changes will benefit my employees. The goal was to get my staff to buy into my culture—and that wouldn't happen if they didn't see an upside.

3. Target key employees.

While neither of them was technically in a position of authority, Everett and Alec seemed to wield greater influence over the others, at least emotionally and spiritually. I would have to make an effort to make them the champions of this new culture. If they bought in, then the entire staff would follow suit. I worried that Alec might be resistant; would I have to part ways with him if he didn't buy in? Could his non-cooperation threaten the entire process? I would have to cross that bridge when I came to it.

4. Celebrate success.

It would be essential to acknowledge and reward progress. It seemed only natural to start with Tommy for helping me out with the collapse. Implementing this culture would require a major shift in workplace procedures and attitude. If I didn't reward progress, my employees could slip back into old habits.

5. Hire for culture.

This would certainly be a bit down the road, but I knew that someday I would be expanding. Not everyone thought like me or had the same work ethic or was necessarily willing to learn, so next time I hired, first and foremost I had to make sure that the applicant could fit into the culture. Only then would I look at their skills and experience.

6. Live the culture.

Culture isn't just a list of rules and expectations. On the job, it needed to be a way of life. Once the culture was built, it would largely be self-sustaining, but until then, the onus would be on me and my management to actually live it. If any of my staff saw me disregard the values I was preaching, the new culture would be written off as nothing more than a hypocritical decree.

Now I had my plan. I figured it would take the next few months for it to solidify in practice.

It was now noon. I had been working since eight. My three-month outline wasn't entirely filled in, but I felt good and clear about it. So now it was off to do cleanup work the rest of the day—and begin the rebuilding process.

At the Corro house, I grabbed a few towels and some window washing fluid. I knew that cleaning the glass panel would take several hours. While washing away the mud and filth, I couldn't help but think about my plan.

What if I couldn't trust my employees to buy into this new culture?

What if they wouldn't be candid about their issues?

What if I couldn't be candid with them?

How would my managers be accountable to my employees, and vice versa? Could they all be accountable to each other?

Could I do what I say I was going to do? Might I accidentally corrupt this newfound culture I desired—again?

The more mud I wiped off the panel, the more doubt clouded my mind. But then, inside me somewhere, I heard an echo of Vern's voice: keep your employees engaged and interested in their work. Perhaps I hadn't lost him after all.

I remembered reading about employee engagement and a concept in which the author described how employees who work with passion feel a profound connection to their company. By most estimates, experts consider only thirty percent of employees to be engaged. Having all my employees engaged didn't seem possible, but maybe there was a way to get pretty darn close to it.

When Vern and I had last spoken, we had talked about marketing. With my customers, my marketing skills were rudimentary, but maybe I could apply my limited talents to my employees. What if I held fast to my company brand: innovation, consistency, and quality? Certainly if I expected my staff to buy into my brand, then I needed to reinforce it to them. How could I expect them to be strong and consistent if I wasn't? I had to be a steady guide, like the North Star. I had to prove I could be innovative, and I had to allow them to do the same. I had to demand quality leadership from myself and let the idea trickle down.

But what if they didn't agree? One hallmark of marketing is asking for feedback from customers. Right? What if I did the same with my employees? Brilliant! Not only would it make them feel valued and appreciated, but they might have good insight as well! Perhaps new construction techniques, materials, ideas! It was a two-way street after all, and I had learned my lesson with communication once before; now I must take it to the next level.

But how could I expect valuable feedback if my employees didn't feel engaged? I thought that maybe I should invest in their career development. Everett, for example, was a brilliant innovator. He built models and tested new ideas. It'd be great to clone him—and he wasn't a carpenter or an architect. I could help him get his carpenter license and even subsidize his schooling for architecture. Imagine what he could become—and he'd feel more attached to me and my business.

Let's see, what else could I do? Tommy had a difficult personal life, and I rarely sat down and discussed it with him. Perhaps I could help him in some small way. He was one of my most successful accidents. I couldn't afford to lose him, so I needed to invest in him.

As for everyone else, I would have to tailor their experience, that is, I would make every effort to ensure that they were both challenged and fulfilled by their job, by Jack's Modern Design, and by me.

Was this too unconventional? Who cared—I was convinced! I needed to market to my employees just like I needed to with my customers. I would find that they were more engaged and more productive than ever. If their enthusiasm, like a smile, was contagious, then the net result would mean a better experience for my employees, my managers, myself, and ultimately my customers. Win-win, right?

After a few hours of careful wiping, I checked my work. Yes! The panel had cleaned up perfectly. And, to say the least, I was amazed by how such a disaster could inspire new ideas.

Now for the rubble. I looked over all the concrete and plaster strewn across the hill. I grabbed a broom and rake and leaned into the task of cleaning up the entire slope. I filled up the dumpster to the brim, and as I wrapped up, I could hardly fit in any more trash.

I made it home by six that night—a full day's work. Tomorrow I would talk with my employees about my idea of culture. What could go wrong? I had a foundation for a company culture, I had a three-month plan that was evolving into a three-year plan, and I had a new strategy to engage my staff. I was a little worried, though. Failure was always possible, it seemed. And it wouldn't be simple to maintain a positive culture: as the boss, as a leader, the culture right now hung entirely on me.

That night I lay down in bed and looked over at Erica. She was already asleep. Her lovely face nestled cozily on a down pillow. Making her happy was all I had ever wanted to do in my life. All she really wanted was the simple pleasure of a family. Before marrying her, you could say I might have been resigned to an ordinary life of working a job and just getting by. Erica made me want more. Neither of us dreamed of being wealthy; we were happy as long as we got a paycheck, the bills got paid, there was a roof over our heads, and food was on the table. But what about having a family? Could we really provide for kids? Could we make them happy?

I had started Jack's Modern Design so that we could live that life. Have a family. Guarantee my family's wellbeing and happiness. It was always about more them than me, even though I may sometimes forget that. I had lost my passion several times simply because I felt burned out. In fact, looking at Erica tonight I realized it had been a long time since I remembered how much more I wanted from life. I wanted to be an entrepreneur, not just an employee of my own business.

Plan in mind, action in heart, and body in action, I would reform JMD—no, not JMD; *Jack's Modern Design*. My name was on the company. Once in a while, we would shorthand it, but I owned *Jack's Modern Design*, not for just me, but for her and for our family.

Family. Engagement. Passion. I realized my family didn't just end in blood. Tommy had done right—he was family. I wouldn't be where I was without Vern—he was family. My entire staff, they worked diligently for me—they were family. Could they possibly betray my values? If they did, they might have to change or leave. If any of my employees betrayed my company, my values, my beliefs, my life, then they could either rectify that or leave!

Slow down! I was tired. My thoughts were like a runaway freight train speeding away on its own. Stop thinking negatively. Everyone would buy in. After all, that's why I strategized. Of course, there might come a time when I would have to seriously consider some negative possibility, but, for now, everyone got the thumbs up. For now, everyone in my life would be family, whether by blood or by business. I would protect them and bring them up to be successes.

I had come close to defeat, but I would not bow. Now I had the strategy. Now I had my plan. And now I would succeed. I took a personal blood oath in my mind: *Now would be my time.*

# Chapter 11
# CHANGES

That next morning I woke up feeling groggy. I had worked late cleaning up the mess, and every fiber of my body felt strained. A cold sweat glued me to the sheets, but I managed to peel myself out of bed and glanced out the window. It was cold and gray. I saw a bit of frost crawling up the window. It was too early in the summer for frost.

I didn't want to go to the job site today—I just ached too much. Besides, there were a lot of other things to get done. Today was about rebuilding. Yesterday I had created a plan and cleaned up the Corro site. Those were the easy parts. Implementing the rest of the changes, especially at such a critical moment, would be exceptionally difficult.

Even though I would have liked to stay home, I actually did have to go out to the Corro house. I had to sit down with each one of the crew and let him know that Jack's Modern Design would now become a "team-oriented, non-competitive environment, with a focus on getting the job done to near-perfect quality." My biggest concern was that they might assume I was making changes because of something they did. But whatever anyone might have done, I was still the leader. I just needed to make sure that Tommy was on board. If things went well with him, then I would have nothing to worry about with the others. I would talk with Lisa at a later time.

I got dressed and started out for the site, it felt like "the long road ahead."

Arriving at the Corro house, I went inside. On the second floor, Tommy was chatting with the Funar brothers. They didn't notice me, so I eavesdropped on their conversation.

"So he came all the way up here without question?" Daniel asked.

"Yep," Tommy replied. "Even bought me dinner after we dragged that entire thing out of the water."

"Nice of him, huh? How long did it take you two to get that thing out?"

"An hour and a half or so."

The tone of their voices sounded positive, and Tommy seemed to be upbeat about how I assisted him.

I announced my presence with, "Hey, Tommy! Mind if we speak for a few moments?"

"Sure thing, Jack." He turned to the Funar brothers. "Get back to work you two," he instructed, cheerfully, before walking over to me. "So what is it you need, Jack?" he asked.

"Bear with me for a moment, OK?" I said, a little nervously, "I think we need to make some significant changes to the way Jack's Modern Design operates."

"Oh boy, this sounds serious. This wouldn't have to do with the collapse, would it?"

"Yes, it does, and other things as well."

"Are we firing anyone?"

"I certainly hope not, but I couldn't say for sure."

"OK, go on. Exactly what changes are you talking about?"

"Mostly team structures. No one directly oversees our second team. You kind of do, but you are already busy with the first team."

"You mean Everett and the twins?"

"Yes," I said. "And Alec from time to time."

The second team, as Tommy and I often called them, was a group of carpenters who only had a couple of years' experience. Overall, they were assigned the most basic tasks and rarely worked with our specialized materials. They were a hard working group and always got the job done. Tommy and I rarely had to intervene or check their work. Until now, I didn't think they needed a manager.

"Well," replied Tommy, "so far the guys on the second team always seem to just do what they're told. None of their jobs are ever too complicated."

"You're right," I said, "but now I want all my staff reporting and giving feedback to managers, and the managers to me. That way we can give them the necessary feedback and award success and attempt to prevent failures."

"Could be a tall order, Jack. But I think your best bet is Kurt. Overall, he has the most experience as a carpenter, and the boys usually turn to him for advice on projects. He does good work and is already like the director of that crew."

Kurt was an older man, a carpenter of nearly twenty years' experience. From what I recall when I hired him, he never changed companies from when he was first hired. He came to us when he realized his previous firm was about to go under. While he was always on top of his work and frequently assisted the others when they were unsure about their tasks, I had never seen him actually manage anyone.

"I don't think he has much management experience, Tommy. Do you think you could teach him some of what you have learned?"

"Sure thing. But are you certain he will accept the position?"

"What do you mean?" I asked.

"Well, I remember when you first asked me to be a full-time manager and how it seemed overwhelming. I mean, I got through it fine, and I hope I've done a good job, but some days it still feels just like... well, just a lot. I'm not sure how Kurt will react."

"He seems like our best bet, though. Even if he might not turn out to be management material, if we don't give him a chance to try we'll never know."

Tommy chuckled. "A few months ago I would never have expected to hear *that* coming out of your mouth."

I laughed, too. "Yeah, things do change."

"All right. So what else is on the agenda?"

"First things first," I said. "We've got to let everyone know the expectations."

"Should I do that?"

"No. If we were a larger company, I'd probably want you to, but I think it will mean more coming from me. Just let me know when each team has about fifteen minutes when I can talk to them individually."

"OK. Got it."

Tommy went off to figure out the times while I went down to the lake for a moment to collect my thoughts. I stood and gazed out over the lake. An early season snow had created a white peak on the distant mountain.

Helping my guys see the benefits of my new approach seemed like the greatest challenge. For some, this would be easy because I knew they genuinely cared about the company's success. But I didn't know if others were that interested. Only time would tell.

I walked into the half-constructed home through the gaping hole that was the focus of everyone's work. Tommy flagged me down. "Hey, Jack, we are pretty busy working on these repairs, but I figured out some time with each man in a way that we can keep on schedule. Daniel's up first."

I took a deep breath. *No getting out of this.* "All right. I'll pull him aside."

Beginning with Daniel, I was gratified and relieved that the conversations went very well. I told each of my staff the new expectations, and no one seemed defensive. The twins were satisfied there would be more two-way communication, and they also seemed happy with the idea of increasing productivity. Both of them were already good workers and weren't looking for things to be easy anyway.

Kurt was both intrigued and apprehensive about my proposal to make him a manager. I told him he had already demonstrated leadership with his team and that Tommy had been very much like him when he first started. "And look how phenomenal Tommy turned out!" I said.

I could tell Kurt was pleased by the way he replied with, "Sure, I'll give it a shot."

Everett was fine with all the changes—bored, even. But boy did he perk up when I mentioned that I would like him to get his carpentry license and that the company would subsidize his course work for certification. I figured it was a win-win proposition: I would get a certified highly skilled carpenter who could be a loyal, long-term employee, and Everett would get a career. He seemed happy with the deal, and as he left our meeting, he vowed to work harder. He kept thanking me until I had to shoo him off back to work. It was nice how grateful he felt, and it gave me hope that these changes would be for the better.

My last conversation was with Alec. It was toward the end of the day. I searched through the building looking for him and finally found him sitting upstairs, texting away on his phone.

"Hey, Alec, mind if I speak with you briefly?"

He quickly tucked away his phone. "I swear, Jack, I was just texting my mother." His voice slightly trembled.

"No, it is not about that at all," I began and then paused. "Well, it sort of is. Follow me outside for a minute." As we marched downstairs, I could sense Alec's rapid breathing behind me. We made our way to the pool and stood by the concrete edge overlooking the lake. The tranquility of the view seemed to calm him down a bit.

"So Alec, I just wanted to let you know that we are making a few changes around here."

"Uh, OK. What kind of changes?"

"Well, you are going for your MBA, aren't you? So you must have heard of the term 'company culture,' right?"

He nodded. He was staring out over the lake and seemed to be quickly becoming detached.

I continued, "So we are trying to foster a more team-oriented environment with a focus on high-quality work."

Alec jerked his head around to look at me and snapped, "And my work hasn't been high quality? Is that what you're trying to say? Do you blame me for the collapse, too?"

"Hang on, Alec, you got this all wrong. I'm not blaming anyone for the collapse. Why would I blame you?"

"Never mind. It doesn't matter. I just assumed that's why you wanted to talk with me. Some of the guys just seem irritated with me a lot of the time, so I figured everyone would blame me for the collapse as well."

"Ah, I see. Well, I'm sorry to hear that. So far you have contributed well, but some of the guys might be a tad irked because while they are laboring away, they can see you either texting or playing games on your phone."

"But it is because I have nothing to do! I mean, what *am* I supposed—"

I held up my hand, interrupting him. "If you can try to help out the other guys, I'm sure they'd appreciate it."

"But I'm no carpenter. Besides, you didn't hire me to do grunt work! I'm an idea man and training to be a manager; can't I do that instead?"

I didn't know if I liked the way he said "grunt work," and his whole tone may have been out of line, but I couldn't be sure if he really knew what he was saying. In any case, to account for my own anxiousness at that moment, I thought I would give him the benefit of the doubt.

I responded, "So you can't, say, help pick up tools and clean up a little at the end of the work day? Also, if you must text someone or take a break, simply slip away, so everyone isn't aware of what you are doing. And learning something about carpentry from the guys will give you a deeper understanding of architecture. Look at it as an opportunity to increase your knowledge while you get paid! There are any number of things you can do. But remember, work is for work."

Alec sighed, then said off-handedly, "Fine, fine. I'll give it a shot."

I sent him off to continue his work for the day, but his attitude reverberated in my mind. I convinced myself it was nothing but just a kid having a bad day. Walking back in the building, I saw Alec and Everett chatting. At first, I was concerned and started walking toward them, but then I saw Everett point to the wall as if explaining something. I left them alone and went off to do some menial work; after talking all day, it felt good to de-stress by just swinging a hammer.

A deep red glow from behind the mountain peak signaled the end of the day. I watched my staff sweep up and put away equipment, then headed for my little Nissan. Just as I was about to drive off, Tommy ran over, huffing and saying, "Jack, we've got a problem."

*What on earth? Not another one!* "OK, what's happened now?" I said in exasperation.

"It's Everett. I don't know why, but he was talking to the twins and saying he is thinking about quitting!"

"What the heck do you mean? I spoke to him earlier, and he seemed grateful to be working here. What happened? What is going on?"

"I don't know, Jack. I just now heard it from the twins and ran to catch you before you left."

"Has Everett left?" I glanced around. Stupid question. His car was right next to mine.

"No. I think he is inside talking to Alec right now."

I hurried over to the house and looked in through the doorframe. I saw Everett sitting on a sawhorse on the upstairs landing, talking to Alec. I waved at him and called out, "Everett, come on down, I have to talk with you." I noticed Everett look at Alec, who gave him a slight nod.

I stood on the ground floor and had Everett sit on one of the bottom stairs. I didn't want to tower over him, but I needed answers. I was the boss, but I still needed him to be relaxed. I went straight to the point, "Everett, Tommy tells me you are talking about quitting. What's up?"

"Well, that's not it exactly."

"Then what is it?"

"The last time things went bad you came down pretty hard on us. We've got another mess to clean up now, and despite the changes you say you are going to make, I don't feel I can do what's going to be necessary without . . ." He hesitated.

I filled in the blank: "Let me guess—a bonus."

He blushed, nodded, and looked down at the floor.

"And what about the positive aspects of the change, rewarding success?" I asked. "You've been a good carpenter, and I intend to help you get your license. Have you forgotten that?"

"No, it's just . . ." He gulped.

"Everett, what exactly happened to convince you that the changes are going to turn out for the worse?"

His glance darted around as though he was following an invisible fly. He finally said, "It was Alec. I was telling him about the last time you made changes, and how it led to you nearly pushing all of us away, and how you got us back on track by offering everyone a bonus. Also,

I told him I thought the collapse was kind of caused by everything that happened during that period."

"Sure. I understand. But I thought I explained to you that the changes, this time, were for the better? Didn't you understand why that would be?"

"Yeah, sort of, but Alec convinced me that if I wasn't given proper assurances, then I should probably consider working elsewhere."

"Listen, Everett, if you really don't trust me and feel you need to look elsewhere, that's fine. But the problem was that I screwed up. I have learned a hard lesson. I drove you guys too hard, and now the building is half collapsed—that's $100,000 out of my pocket for the repairs. Now I'm trying to change systems so that never happens again—not just so I don't lose money, but so you guys can grow and develop as better employees. Sometimes that means bonuses, but not bonuses for the wrong reasons. Bonuses for success!"

"All right, Jack, I get it. I'll think about what you said. I mean, I think you're right, and I'm sorry I forgot about your offer to help. I am grateful. I'm just a little confused right now."

"That's fine, Everett. Give yourself a day or so and we can talk whenever you are ready."

Everett was a good employee. I knew he'd be fine. But now I was really pissed at Alec and had to deal with him. Vern and I had never talked much about the type of conflict Alec seemed to be generating, and, despite his decent work, I was already half-settled on cutting him loose. Firing someone was always difficult, and I would prefer to turn the situation around, but I also knew that wasn't always possible.

I wasn't sure how to weigh the pros and cons of doing it. I tried to think it through.

Could we talk through the issues? I knew that whenever I had an underperforming employee, the first thing to do was sit down and talk through the issues. I had let Alec know that he wasn't living up to expectations. Maybe I should have asked if there was anything that I could do to help that.

Did I help re-energize him? I knew that the performance of employees often decreased because they had lost interest in their jobs. To turn this around, it was good to try to re-engage them in the operation. There were many ways of going about this, including simply listening to their concerns and doing one's best to address them. If they felt like their talents weren't being utilized in their current position, you could consider adjusting their job description to allow them to spend more time doing what they were best at. I had done this, but Alec felt that there was only so much time he could tolerate "grunt work."

Had I followed up with him regularly? Once an employee has begun to underperform, you need to monitor the situation closely—this was part of my failure. It is possible for an unhappy individual to sabotage the morale of an entire team, and this was something I couldn't afford. Once I had spoken to Alec, I would need to see clear improvement or I simply couldn't keep him around. The trouble was, I already caught him slacking and had just spoken to him about it not an hour earlier. Sure, I didn't do everything I possibly could have, but he was now, actively, spreading discontent. A few questions started coming to mind.

*Did Alec respect me?* If not, it was time to let him go. I knew I could turn around poor performance and resolve personal conflicts, but it would be very difficult to make a disrespectful employee respectful.

*Did Alec care about the job?* On the surface, it seemed that way. If he did care, then I could almost certainly find a way to turn things around. If he didn't, there would be nothing I could do besides cut ties. It is impossible to get through to somebody who simply doesn't care.

*Did I actually trust Alec?* Trust is critical to building a winning team. If I couldn't be sure about Alec, then I might have to let him go simply for that. I had made that mistake in the past, so I wanted to tread lightly with this and make sure I wasn't overreacting.

I asked myself: "When I hired Alec, if I knew what I know now, would I have hired him?" A good question, but I wasn't too sure about my answer. If it was going to be "yes," then maybe I could still work with him. If it turned out to be "no," then he would have to go.

I had found out that most of the time the cause of an employee problem actually rested with the manager, who happened to be me. I had made one or more of these mistakes: I had hired the wrong person, didn't train him properly, didn't provide adequate direction, or didn't provide adequate resources. But in this case, I couldn't be sure what I had done wrong. Maybe it was simply an attitude problem. I would find out soon enough.

I marched upstairs to meet with Alec. He was sitting on the sawhorse where he had been talking with Everett. His tools, which he could have easily picked up and put away, were scattered all around him. He was texting on his phone.

"Alec," I said, "we need to talk."

"Again boss? We already chatted today."

I felt my face starting to flush. "Everett tells me you've been saying some things about me and Jack's Modern Design. Mind telling me about that?"

"Oh that. Pfff, it was nothing. I just said that since you had screwed up, which led to the wall collapsing, you shouldn't take it out on your employees."

"That's true enough, I'll admit, but you said something about everyone should get raises?"

"Well, you did that in the past, so why shouldn't you do it now since everyone has to pick up your mess?"

"OK, so I'm trying to make some changes now to prevent all of that happening again. I discussed with you some of those changes."

Alec interrupted, "Yeah, some of which require me to do what you didn't hire me for. I'm not going to get my hands dirty. Unlike you, I've got a college degree."

*How oblivious was this kid?* I wondered. I desperately wanted to give him a chance, but he kept digging himself into a deeper and deeper hole. I felt my face flushing more and more red. I had to ask him directly, "Tell me, Alec, do you even respect what I do, what my business does?"

"Now Jack that seems like a loaded question."

"What the hell does that mean?" I was about to explode.

"Well, I respect the work I'm trying to do here, and I like seeing things that I suggest, getting carried out; that is why I'm going for my MBA. But you, as a boss, parading as an architect? I mean, seriously! Some of the work you have done is certainly nice, but you are just not an architect; that's why you hired me."

That was it! Alec had confirmed my suspicions. I had to cut him loose. "Alec, it's clear you don't respect me or my decisions, so I'm sorry, but I am letting you go. I'll accept your two-week notice rather than taint your record by firing you."

I turned my back and headed downstairs; I had said my piece, and there was nothing more I could do. When I stepped out the door, I saw my staff packing up for the day and saying their farewells to each other. I waved as they were getting into their cars.

"Hey! Not so fast!" Alec shouted.

I turned around. Alec was standing in the doorway. I shuddered.

"You think you can just fire someone because of their attitude? What's it got to do with me that you don't run a tight enough ship to get the results you want? Are you going to fire anyone just because they don't agree with you? Pathetic!"

I was way over the edge now. "Alec! I was going to let you leave peacefully, but if you show your face here again, I'm calling the cops! I never want to see you again!"

"Yeah, right. You think I'm the only one? Everett agrees with me, don't you, Everett?" Alec pointed over my shoulder. I turned around. Everyone was still here, a small crowd of astonished faces.

Everett's mouth was agape. He stuttered his response, "No, Alec. You ought to just go. I can't believe I listened to you in the first place."

Alec's righteously angry expression fell from his face in disbelief. "What did you say?"

Everett opened the door of his car before turning back toward Alec and saying, "Just go away."

The rest of the crew got in their cars and drove away. By now my anger had dissipated. I looked at him and calmly said, "Alec, go home." I watched him slowly make his way to his car.

I couldn't help but wonder how everyone would react—not only to the changes but to Alec's outburst, and my first firing, a public one at that. No entrepreneur is perfect, and even the largest companies make mistakes, but Alec's attitude was infectious and dangerous.

The best way to keep turnover low is to make each hiring decision carefully. My biggest mistake with Alec was that I didn't do that; I didn't think about how well he would fit in with Jack's and if he would be happy here in the long run. From now on I would have to be diligent: I would call a candidate's previous employers to see if there were any potential problems. Maybe if I'd done that with Alec, I could have identified his lack of respect for authority.

As for my other employees, there were different concepts I could use to prevent them from leaving or having to fire them. For one, I needed to keep them engaged. Part of the reason Everett nearly left was that Alec had convinced him that he was unappreciated. To keep each employee engaged and feeling appreciated, on an ongoing basis I needed to seek their input and offer positive reinforcement.

Another issue I had in the past was overworking them to the point of burnout. It was so tempting to ask for more and more from my employees, especially the really good ones. But that backfired, and I had learned a lesson. Even though they were not complaining at the time, I hadn't been observant enough to notice the signs.

I was now doing some good with the company culture. I was giving everyone the opportunity to grow. Everett had ambitions to become a licensed carpenter, and I intended to help him achieve that. He had mastered his current job, and I was finding him new challenges. As for my other employees, I would have to find similar ways to support their desires to grow and improve themselves. This didn't have to mean moving everyone to different departments or rewriting their job descriptions; simply adding more responsibility might be enough to keep them happy and engaged. The bottom line was that my best employees expected to grow as time passed. They expected more responsibility, fresh challenges, and higher compensation. I would need to develop a long-term plan to keep all my employees happy, and then—and only then—could I be sure they'd be with me for the long haul.

At last, I had my plan for the future. And today, foremost in my mind was keeping my best staff around and preventing incidents like the one that had just occurred. It would be an understatement to say I was nervous about tomorrow. I valued my realization of just how much my company culture was tied to my success—and keeping that culture strong was a powerful tool that I needed to continue to cultivate.

I sorely missed Vern. I thought of a motto to help myself: Keep your attention in the present and let the future lie ahead.

# Chapter 12
# FIREFLY

The next morning I came in early to the Corro house. A heavy ground fog covered the water. I walked to the shore where I noticed a great blue heron standing in the water. The majestic creature seemed unaware of my approach. It was beautifully tranquil. I don't know why, but the whole scene seemed eerie to me. Maybe it was because I was anxious about the staff's possible reaction to the previous day.

I heard the faint sound of a car approaching. The heron noticed and took flight, landing a few hundred feet down the shore. Everett's truck pulled up, and he unpacked his gear. Like the heron, he seemed unaware of my presence. I stood by and watched him work. He didn't look very enthusiastic as he began repairing the gap in the wall. I wondered if his apparent lack of interest had anything to do with last night's incident. Had he really he wanted to quit?

I heard the engine sounds of more cars. It was the twins and Tommy.

Still apparently hidden by the misty shroud, I watched as my lead team set up the new supports for the walls and glass panel. Tommy pointed out to the twins where to get started, and they hustled to work. He then walked over to Everett and gave him a pat on the back; the two shared a brief smile. If anything was wrong, I certainly couldn't tell from here.

As I was approaching the house, my phone rang. Startled by the sound, Everett looked up. He waved, beaming a smile as he did. I waved back, and he returned to work. I looked at my cell phone—it was the office. "Hey Lisa, what's up?"

"Good news, Jack. I made a couple calls, and I think I found us a small job. It's just a kitchen renovation, but it can add to our cash flow for the month and help make up for the—um—setback."

"Thanks, Lisa. That's good. What do they want to be done?" This was a perfect opportunity, I thought, to put Kurt's leadership to the test.

"I'm not sure, but apparently they have a design plan and have already ordered many of the materials."

I thought that was odd. Why would anyone order materials without a carpenter already on the job?

"Do you know how they heard about us?" I asked.

"I'm not entirely sure, but from what I could gather, the husband heard about your work from Dave Cowen."

"You mean our first client?"

"Yes. Anyway, he thought he could rebuild the kitchen himself as a DIY project, and his wife got irritated. I had been calling our previous clients like you told me to do, and Dave referred me to them. The wife seemed pleased by our offer, particularly with the time frame."

This reminded me of some of the projects I had done in my own home and how Erica would complain that I couldn't do it alone because it would take too long. "What time frame did you offer them?"

"Three weeks. With all the materials already on site, I figured it'd only take a week and a half, but I built in some extra time for any issues that might arise."

Three weeks still seemed like a short deadline; if any issues did crop up then Kurt's team would have to react quickly. But, I thought, the challenge might prove him and his team's capabilities. I'd have to give him a bit of instruction on management, though.

"When did they say we could start?" I asked.

"Next Wednesday. Your schedule looked clear for Monday, so I told them we could do it then."

"Hmm, check Kurt's schedule for the coming weeks as well, and his schedule for tomorrow, too."

I heard the click-clack of the keys typing away. Finally, Lisa came back to the phone. "He's available tomorrow and Monday. Should I give him a call?"

"Yeah. Tell him to cancel his plans for Monday and set aside some time tomorrow to speak with me."

"Should I tell him what it's about?"

"No. Just tell him it's good news."

"All righty, will do."

I hung up and went back to the house. Everyone was hustling around, repairing the gaping hole. Their work was impressive—in the time I was on the call the team had put up the supports and had started the second story flooring. They had done enough that I could no longer walk directly to the shore through the hole in the wall. I went through the front entrance and saw Tommy taking a breather. He let out a bellowing laugh as I approached.

"Boy, you really got the jump on Everett earlier!" he said.

I looked at him, puzzled. "That certainly wasn't my intention."

"Ha! I know, and Everett does too. Apparently you really made him jump. The twins have been joking around with him about it ever since.

He claims that he didn't even know you were here, and the twins were like, 'What? You didn't notice his car?' I don't know, but it is certainly giving me a laugh."

"I can tell. They're not too hard on him, are they?"

"Nah. It seemed like it's all in good fun, or I would have stopped it."

"That's good. A little bit of fun is always OK, as long as it is not at anyone's expense. Anyways, I was hoping you could join me tomorrow when I speak with Kurt."

"Kurt? What about?"

"Well, I need to explain a bit about management to him. We've got a new job starting next week, and I need him to oversee it."

"Next week, hmm. That seems rather early for him to be put in that position; you don't just teach management overnight."

"I don't expect he will learn everything in the course of the next few weeks, but let's give him the opportunity. We can keep an eye on him. I just want to give him the basic tools of management and see how he runs with it."

"You don't think it's a bit risky?" asked Tommy.

"The project is fairly routine. Besides, I think we can give him enough advice to make things go smoothly."

"And you want me to share my advice? I'm not such a great manager."

"Quit humbling yourself, Tommy. You and the team get along well, and, more importantly, they respect you."

"And that's why you fired Alec?"

I held my breath for a moment. I knew this question was bound to come up sooner or later, and I didn't know how I would react. Then I thought, *why am I conflicted about this?* I needed to follow the rules that I had written for Jack's company culture and speak the plain truth. "Yes, that was the main reason."

Tommy didn't bat an eye. He just continued with, "Humph. A few of the guys were wondering what his outburst was all about."

"Oh? And how do they feel about it?"

"Well, the twins seemed relieved. They had often told me they felt something wasn't quite right with Alec. David told me that some of the things Alec said around him seemed plain old degrading. He didn't know if Alec was being intentionally nasty or not, but he sure thought Alec was too smug for his own good."

"And here I thought I was the only one," I said, relieved. "Any idea why no one said anything?"

"Not really, but from what the twins told me, they weren't sure if Alec was insulting them or not. They just felt uncomfortable and figured it was probably just them, so they didn't say anything."

"That's too bad," I said. "We might have been able to avoid the whole problem, including the outburst."

"Maybe, but who could have predicted that? I mean, Alec trying to call you out in front of everyone! Was that guts or stupidity? And then trying to drag Everett into it? I couldn't believe my ears!"

"Me neither. So how is Everett taking it?"

"I'm not sure. You know, it seemed like he and Alec got along pretty well, and that is probably why he was considering quitting after the two of them spoke. I don't know what you said to him to convince him to stick around, but today he is acting as though nothing happened."

"I'm not so sure that's a good thing."

"You'd have to ask him," said Tommy. "But he has been doing good work today and hasn't indicated that he is interested in leaving."

"That's good. Maybe the whole thing is over with, and we can get on with the project. At least, Alec won't be causing any more problems for us."

"I wouldn't be so sure."

"What do you mean?" I asked, surprised by Tommy's comment.

"I might just be a pessimist, but this was the first time you have fired someone, and, unfortunately, it was very public."

"Yeah. If only we would have caught on sooner."

"I'm sure there could be some 'if only' situations, but so far all is going well."

"I'd rather be counting profits."

"Hey, that'll come. We haven't been doing that badly so far. At least this Corro project is paying well. While I certainly don't know the numbers, it must be helping us. Right?"

I couldn't help but feel bad about the financial situation Jack's was in. I really didn't want to discuss it with the crew, not even Tommy, but I also knew that honesty was the best—no, the *only*—policy. I gave him the quick outline.

"No way," said Tommy, half-shocked. "I would never have guessed, you come in so positive; I had assumed everything was fine."

"How do you think it would affect the crew if I didn't come into work every day in a good mood? Do you think everyone would work just as hard?"

"I think they might even be *more* motivated if they knew how difficult things are. I mean, the guys like you!"

"Maybe, Tommy, but don't let them know how precarious things are, OK? Just keep them focused on their work. I'm looking into a few other projects that can help us out."

"Sure. I know you'll figure it out. For the most part, everyone enjoys working with you, and we like the jobs we've gotten."

I wished I were as positive as Tommy seemed to be, but to me, these were desperate times.

Crash! A loud noise from across the house broke the silence. Tommy jumped up. "Got to run. Sounds like the twins are at something again."

Although part of me still worried about unknown repercussions of having fired Alec, for now, at least, my anxiety was put to rest.

At home that night, I poured over Vern's notes about what makes a good manager. I wondered how I could communicate it to Kurt. Tommy had proven himself a capable manager, so what was he doing, and what does it actually take? Vern had told me before about the difference between management and leadership; his focus with me always had been on good leadership. While there were certain similarities between the two, each role was unique, but Vern and I hadn't thoroughly talked about them.

It was now eleven o'clock. I had been studying and thinking about leadership and management for the better part of three hours. I asked myself the question: Could Kurt learn something from my mistakes? I scribbled down some notes and decided to call it a night; I had my plan for the morning.

The next morning, driving into work, I was nervous about presenting my thoughts on management to Kurt. Until actually doing management, I remember thinking how easy it must be. I certainly learned my lesson on that the hard way. My goal with Kurt was to help him avoid the mistakes I had made.

Even though I arrived at the site bright and early, I wasn't the first one there. Everett was already setting up for his job of the day. He looked up at my little Nissan as I drove in on the dirt path. As I got out of the car, he came over and said, "Hey, Jack, Tommy spoke to me about the whole Alec thing, and he told me that you were concerned about how I acted the other day. I don't know what got into my head, but I just wanted to apologize for my behavior."

"Well thanks, Everett, but don't worry about it. It is fine." Wow, I thought, that was an unexpected surprise. "But you are still going to stick around, right?"

"You bet. Where else would I find an employer willing to help me with my license?"

"How's that going anyway?"

"It should be settled in the next two months. I've been bogged down at home, so it's been a slow process."

"I'm sorry to hear that. At least soon you'll be able to work without someone else having to look over your shoulder the entire time."

"Yeah, there's that . . . and a bonus, right?" He chuckled.

I laughed, too, "In this case, yes—once you are licensed, that is."

I heard the rumbling of a couple of vehicles. It was Tommy and Kurt, each in his own truck. Knowing that Everett was sticking around had eased some of my nervousness. I grabbed my notebook. Tommy and Kurt got out of their trucks. "Hey, Jack!" Tommy called out, "Kurt and I just had breakfast. I let him know about the project and told him a few things I have learned about managing."

I hoped that Tommy hadn't already contradicted anything I was going to say. "Oh yeah? Like what?"

"We mostly talked about remembering that our staff are people," said Tommy, "and even though results matter, keeping in mind that we are not working with a bunch of automatons."

Kurt added, "That seemed relatively obvious to me, of course. I appreciate any advice you can give, but I have had my fair share of bad managers who were only concerned about deadlines and results, and it didn't take long before people just got sick of working with them. How about before we get started on more management tips, you fill me in on the job itself? I figure you're not just upping me into management with some massive project."

"You're right, Kurt," I said. "And from what I gather, it is a fairly cut and dry kitchen project, a failed DIY attempt. So we'll have to do some cleanup as well as see if we can improve the project with any modern construction methods or new ideas."

"Right," said Kurt. "That's what makes Jack's unique and why I was interested in working here in the first place. I mean, I don't know tons about the latest and greatest things on the market, but I was interested in finding out and working with them. Like when I saw that massive panel of glass, I was in awe of its size and width, let alone its durability. For me it is just fun to try new things; it is part of the reason I'm willing to try out being a manager."

"That's good to hear," I said. "On Monday, you'll come in with me to check out this job. You'll start with your team on Wednesday, and we'll see how things go. I might want to keep you as a manager if you do well and if you are also comfortable with it."

"Works for me," said Kurt. "So how about those managing tips?"

"For the most part," I replied, "these will be general concepts, and it seems Tommy already covered the fact that our people aren't robots. You have experienced treatment like that in the past, so hopefully it is self-evident. Now then—I have found three elements that should be in place before you launch any project." I glanced at Tommy. "That means *all* of us."

"What are you looking at me for?" Tommy asked.

"I'm just emphasizing the point," I said. "Now, the first thing we need to keep focused on is *where* we are going, and *why*."

Kurt raised an eyebrow. "So what does that mean, specifically?"

"Basically," I said, "it is about remembering the purpose of our service and product, and knowing our time frames and the details of the project. It is understanding what the customer desires and how that fits in with what we do and how we do it. Tommy has had experience with the difficulty of balancing the two. I'm sure you've heard the expression 'the customer is always right.' Well, that's true only in that the customer knows *what* they want, but they might be clueless about *how* to do it, or have outdated ideas about how. Sometimes a client might expect you to do something a certain way, but you know that isn't the best or optimal approach. You'll have to be able to have a conversation about that. And, in reality, that conversation is what our business is all about."

"Are you saying that the customer can be wrong?" Kurt asked.

"Not exactly," Tommy interjected. "What customers want is what they want. We might talk with them about modifying their goals, or we can help them see a new way to reach them."

"I think I get it," said Kurt. "It is more or less about trying to avoid working weeks on a project only to learn that the customer had something else in mind!"

"OK," I said. "Second, plan before you act. For this kitchen project, in theory, it should be fairly simple. But still, write up a master plan. You are going to have four people working under you, so keep in mind their daily tasks and how that fits into the big picture. Keep an eye on your priorities as they might shift quickly in a fairly fast-paced project like this."

"How much time do we have for this kitchen?" Kurt interjected.

"Three weeks, give or take a few days," I replied.

"That doesn't leave much room for error," he said. "Before I can start planning, we'll have to see the project."

"Also, write down your plan," Tommy jumped in. "It makes it easier to assign the right people to the right job. A written plan helps you keep track of your resources." He paused. "Well, that's my input, and it looks like Everett wants me over at the site, so I'll leave you two." He looked at Kurt and said, "You'll do fine. Don't worry too much," then stood up and walked away.

I looked down at my notes and let out a sigh. This next one I frequently had trouble with. "Now for number three. At this point, you have identified what you are going to do and how you are going to do it. Now you have to *communicate* this information to your team. The best way to communicate your objectives is to set clear expectations. You have to make sure everyone knows who is responsible for specific action items. Let them know the intermediate deadlines—not just the final deadline but the deadlines for the day and whatever other smaller objectives. Take the time to communicate your expectations and urge your team to ask questions if there is anything they don't understand. Remember, just because *you* understand something doesn't mean that *your team* does. Don't take any chances—make sure everyone is on the same page."

"It seems simple enough in theory," said Kurt, "and an obvious thing to do. But it also seems like a lot of two-way communication."

"Yes, and it is completely necessary, just as is effective feedback."

"Feedback?" he said. "I never really thought about that."

"Constructive feedback is very important," I said. "It keeps employees on task and helps them develop their skills and become greater assets for the company. But delivering feedback is a challenge, especially if you are correcting someone; even I have trouble with it. It forces you to walk a fine line between being helpful and constructive and being offensive. I have certainly upset my share of employees, so I understand what can happen. I also understand the temptation to put off what may feel to you like a confrontation. But it is almost always better to just do it because it is your job to make sure things are done right."

"If it just has to do with feedback," asked Kurt, "can't the issue be dealt with later?"

"No," I replied. "Avoiding an issue only makes it worse. When you fail to confront an employee about unacceptable behavior, you are validating it. The employee is aware that you witnessed his behavior, and because you didn't say anything about it, he assumes that it is acceptable. This can start a chain reaction, and the next thing you know, most of your team will be adopting similar bad habits. Don't let poor behavior go unanswered. Address it as soon as possible so that it doesn't spread."

"Like what happened with Alec? He was goofing off with his phone, and then Everett started doing the same thing—not to the same degree as Alec, but still—"

"Exactly," I said. "Think of it this way: would you rather put out the fire now, while it is small and relatively tame, or would you rather put it out six months when it has spread and become impossible to control?"

"Again, like Alec."

"Yes. It wasn't easy to confront him, and I paid the price for letting it go on, but I think I know a means to prevent that kind of thing in the future. I actually learned some good approaches from Tommy."

Kurt perked up. "From Tommy? Let's hear it!"

"For one, focus on positives as well as negatives. If your feedback is always negative, your employees will either start to tune you out, or they'll become discouraged. Always make it clear that you appreciate the hard work your employees put in. Whatever you have to say, make a point of ending the conversation on a positive note."

"So for instance, if I caught Everett on his cell phone, I should let him know what he did wrong and then highlight his productiveness?"

"Something like that," I said. "You'll also want to provide action steps with your feedback. Be specific. Don't beat around the bush or be vague. Tell your employees precisely what you have observed and what you would like to see happen differently. By the end of the conversation, the employee should clearly understand both your expectations and how to deliver on them."

"I don't want to pick on him," said Kurt, "but just as an example let's continue with Everett and his cell phone. If his efficiency was down and I could rightly assume it had to do with him goofing around on his phone, then I would want to let him know I noticed his phone time was affecting his work. We could set up a plan to keep him busy, and I would let him know that I expect focused on the job during work hours."

"I'm sure you'll remember," I said, "to make your comments about the *behavior*, not about the *person*. And you also want to help your team understand the big picture. Don't just tell employees what to do; tell them why it is important. Help them see the purpose behind their actions. That way they can feel how their particular job really matters. Once they grasp the big picture, they'll self-correct because they'll have the goals of our business in mind." And, remember to try and catch them doing things right, more often than you catch them doing things wrong!

"I think I see," said Kurt. "And I think you might have already done that with Everett, right? I mean, no one really knows what transpired between you two before you fired Alec."

"Yes, I did. And it wasn't easy for me. And confronting and firing Alec was far from pleasant. But it had to be done, and for Alec, I waited too long."

"Sounds good. I guess this project will give me a chance to practice. I'll try following your advice, and I'll give you a call if I have any issues."

"Cool," I said. "Let's get back to work. Oh, and don't forget to bring a notepad on Monday." We went back to our separate tasks.

I was very satisfied with Kurt's responses and sincerely hoped he could follow through; the new project would certainly be a good test. And even if Kurt wasn't management material, at least, I would find out that I needed to find someone who was.

On Monday, Kurt and I arrived at the kitchen project. While, in their attempt at construction, our new clients had gotten in over their heads, they hadn't done anything seriously wrong, and they had successfully ordered almost all the necessary materials. Kurt impressed me right away with the way he jumped in and asked the clients detailed questions about their desires for the project and then talked about how we might be able to improve the project. For the most part, the design was set in stone, but Kurt and I came up with a few techniques that would expedite the process and make our three-week time frame realistic.

Now I had an idea of where Jack's Modern Design was going, and I had multiple teams working towards the same objectives. Certainly there would be challenges, but I had my plans written down, and nothing was going to get in my way. I knew setbacks would occur, but I would face them. I had learned that, among other things, the power of positive thinking was my greatest ally.

# Chapter 13
# IDENTITY

A s the days passed, everything seemed to be moving along smoothly. Kurt was managing the kitchen project and was nearly always ahead of schedule. His adaptation to being a manager, however, had some problems. Kurt was closer to his team when he started; they would have called each other friends instead of just colleagues. In dealing with their problems, he found the closeness difficult. At that moment, it wasn't much of an issue, but I thought I might later rearrange the teams, so he didn't have to worry about this conflict of interest.

Midway through the kitchen project, Jim, one of the part-time carpenters on Kurt's team, decided to quit. He claimed it was because he was moving out of state. He was a good man, and both Kurt and I were distraught by his departure. Kurt was upset because it happened soon after he took over his team. I could tell he worried that it might have been because of him. As far as I could ascertain, though, Jim's leaving wasn't Kurt's fault. It was just bad timing.

The kitchen job finished on time. Kurt had proven he could handle the challenge of managing his own projects with a team. The Corro project was wrapping up nicely; the accident only set us back a month. I had explained to Chris Corro what had happened, and because we had cleaned up everything and were still doing good work, he let our time frames slide.

We had another month's work to totally finish the Corro house. What would be next for Jack's? I had spent so much time trying to break even that I had lost sight of the future. We had no more jobs after this. What would my staff do? None of us could afford not to work. I called Lisa, "Hey, Lisa, how's it going with getting new leads?"

"Nothing special, Jack, just a few small jobs that might take one or two of the guys. The payoff wouldn't be that great, either."

"Nothing bigger through our previous jobs?"

"No, nothing, I wish we could clone Chris Corro and build tons more houses like his! The perfect client: good payoff and flexible!"

Of course! I thought to myself: Clone Corro. That's it! Not literally, but there's bound to be other people out there like him. But how could we find them? Inspired by Lisa comment, I told her, "Lisa, I need to talk with you in person to discuss our marketing strategy. Can we meet for lunch tomorrow?"

"Sure," she said.

I had set up our meeting for the same coffee shop where Vern and I used to talk. Walking into the shop, the familiar smell of dark roast wafting by my nose put me at ease. I could easily imagine Vern stepping through the door in his overcoat and fedora. I ordered a latté before taking a seat in my usual chair, where I could watch the door for Lisa's arrival. I started to stare into my coffee, watching the milky foam swirl around. Last time I sat in this seat was with Vern, but this time, the answers wouldn't just come to me on his scribbled on sheets of paper. This time, I would have to discover them for myself.

The bell on the door tinkled as Lisa and her assistant, Erin, entered. Erin worked on our website design and helped Lisa with bookkeeping. From what I had seen, she was well organized and very good at her job. I wonder why Lisa had brought her along.

I stood up and borrowed a third chair from a nearby table for Erin. They waved back then exchanged a few words between themselves. Lisa came over and sat down.

"Hi, Jack," Lisa said, smiling. "Erin's ordering our coffee and some sandwiches. Would you like anything?"

"Thanks, but I'm good. I generally don't eat lunch."

"Suit yourself. So why this meeting? I know it's about marketing, but why did you want to meet in person?"

"Well, I wanted to discuss our marketing strategy and see if we could come up with a way to get more clients like Chris Corro."

"Ah, well it's good that I brought Erin, she has been helpful with marketing ideas in relation to the website. After all, I'm principally the bookkeeper."

Huh? How did I get so out of touch with the office? "I thought you were doing the marketing," I said. "You know, making the calls to previous clients looking for leads."

"That's right," said Lisa. "I've been making the calls and doing the leg work, but Erin has helped me by setting up a dialogue and coming up with ideas for an email update every month or so about new projects we are working on."

That's a relief; I thought to myself, at least, I was clear about who was doing which work in the office. "Has Erin given you any insight about how we can get more customers like Mr. Corro?"

"No, she is not sure what to do. She wasn't hired for marketing, just for developing the website. She knows how to use the website for advertising, but so far her results have only led to a couple of small leads."

Erin joined us.

"Hi, Erin, you brought your tablet, right?" I asked. She nodded and pulled out her tablet computer, quickly typed in her password, and handed me the machine. I brought up our website. I scanned it to see if I thought anything was wrong.

The website was very simple; it outlined what we were about and what made us unique. On the left-hand side was a registration for a free quote via email. Everything looked sound. Perhaps there was more to our marketing I would have to explore.

I let out a long sigh and slid the tablet back over to her.

"So what do you think?" she asked me.

"It is a good site when I look at it, but clearly it is not yielding the results we want. Small jobs are fine, but right now we need a job, at least the size of the hotel or Corro project."

"That's a tall order," Erin said. "Maybe we should consider bringing in a specialized marketer. I've got website design skills; I just don't have the experience to hunt down large clients."

Lisa's eyes widened as she responded almost angrily, "We can't afford a marketer. The fact is, we need a big job just so we can keep everyone around here in their own job!"

I held up my hand to intervene. Lisa was clearly upset by what the books had been telling her. I tried to mediate. "If we landed the big jobs on a regular basis I'd gladly pay for a marketer, but we don't have the money and we need a new job now, not tomorrow."

Erin sipped at her coffee. "OK, so maybe we should step back for a moment. Clearly the website is not reaching the right people; so who are the right customers?"

Lisa looked up at the ceiling and let out a groan. I understood how she felt. She and I had never really sat down to discuss who the right customer was. I thought out loud, "Well, Chris has been a great customer. So what makes him great for us?"

Lisa groaned again, sat back up, and looked at her coffee cup. "For one, he's loaded."

Erin rolled her eyes. "Well, that's an obvious advantage."

"Yes," I said. "We need clients who have projects that are large enough to support our company. It is always better to do one big house project than three little kitchen projects. The fee is higher, and the margin is higher."

Erin's eyes lit up as she started typing some notes. "That's good, it's a start."

I continued, "Also, the client would be willing to listen to new ideas and have them incorporated into his project. Thus far, Chris has given fairly positive praise of our work. Lisa, you talked to him not to long ago, would you agree with that?"

"I'd say so," she said. "The only trouble is, he doesn't seem to know anyone looking for the kind of work we do."

"Perhaps that's because he doesn't fully understand what we do," I said.

Erin popped in with, "What do you mean?"

"Well, think about it for a second; he only knows us from building his home. Does he know we also do renovations and home improvement?"

"I assume he knows that," Lisa stated, unfazed.

"Hold on," Erin blurted, "why would he know everything we do? Have we told him about any of our other projects? I don't think we can expect him to know everything about us. It's not like he works here."

"I think we understand what we like about Chris," I said. "Let's talk about it a little more. It would certainly be good to use him for possible referrals and references, but I don't think we can just rely on him for our jobs."

"And so . . . ?" Lisa and Erin asked simultaneously.

"We like that Chris has money and appreciates the quality and innovation we provide," I continued. "How can we reach more clients like him? Can we find a means to advertise directly to them? Where do Chris and people like him hang out? Where do they live? Where would they like to live?"

"How do we gather that information?" Erin asked.

Lisa had seemed bored but now snapped back, "Generally, I would say we could take a look at sales records. But our list is fairly small, so it shouldn't take long to sift through and find our top selling ideas. We've already checked our customer information records, so perhaps we could survey our previous customers and see if we can branch out to any associates, friends, or family."

"Good," I said, smiling. It seemed we were finally on track. "So once we gather that information, we'll need to find ways to reach our best potential customers, whether that be by physical addresses, telephone numbers, or email addresses. In order to get their attention, we'll also need to figure out their 'demographic location,' such as which communication channels they pay most attention to." I paused to let Erin catch up on her note-taking before continuing. "Once we know how to reach them, we'll need to find a way to attract them to us. Since we are looking for wealthy clients with upscale tastes, we'll need to let them know that 'upscale' is what we do."

"It could take us a while to get this information together," Lisa said, "and even if we find new customers, they could be as far away or farther than the Corro project. How would that work?"

"That's fine," I said. "Our top-tier customers with big and possibly newer projects could easily live far away, especially on the lakes of New Hampshire. For renovations, however, we might want to look in the Boston area where new homes aren't being built as often, but where a lot of renovation happens."

Erin let out a little hum. I glanced at her. "Um, it's nothing," she said as if I were going to ask her what she was thinking. "Just give me a second." She continued typing away on her tablet.

Lisa asked, "Do we know, though, that our core customer market is big enough? How strong is the competition already targeting them? Are you sure we'll be able to affordably reach them? Marketing can be expensive, right?"

"That's a good reality check we are going to have to do," I replied. "It might not be possible to reach our top-tier customers, or it might be too costly. We might have to go after our second- or third-tier customer."

"All right, assuming we can gather this information, then what?" Lisa asked.

"Then we'll have a solid grasp of our best customer profile," I said. "We have to take some action steps, but currently, we don't know which direction to go."

Erin let out a low grumble. She was obviously doing more than just taking notes on that tablet.

"I think I have an idea," she said. "I remember when Chris Corro spoke to Lisa, he said that a bunch of people across the lake from him had been buying up properties and tearing down the old structures on them."

"You never mentioned this, Lisa," I said as I raised an eyebrow and looked at her.

"Sorry, Jack," Lisa blushed. "We were repairing the Corro house at the time. It came up in one of my brief conversations with Chris. I guess I forgot."

"Yeah, that was a hectic period." I looked at Erin and asked, "Is there anything we can do to reach those people?"

"Let's see here," she said as she poked and swiped at the screen of her tablet. "OK, here we go. It looks like there are a few open house showings taking place in one of the lakeside towns. In fact, there's one next Sunday. I read in the paper about all the rebuilding happening over there. Perhaps if we go to this next open house, we might be able to mingle and get the lay of the land."

"Can you go, Lisa?" I asked.

"I have plans with my husband, but I think Erin's probably got a better grasp on this than I do."

I turned to Erin. "What do you think? Are you up for this?"

"Of course—and besides, it says right here on their advertisement that they're serving free appetizers," she said with a grin.

"All right then," I said. "Erin and I will go. In the meantime, can you two gather a bit of information on how we can advertise to them, pique their interest?"

"Well, we can get something together," Lisa replied. "It might not be as complete as we'd like, given the time frame, but it will be useful." She pulled out a calendar and added, "I might have to pull an extra shift on Saturday, though, to do it."

"Great! At least, we have a plan now," I said, satisfied that we had done our best. "We'll see how it pans out."

After a few days of wondering and worry and a flurry of emails zipping between Lisa, Erin, and myself, we finally settled on a few selling points. Lisa had collected testimonials from a few of our previous clients, including Chris, and Erin worked them into a small pamphlet we could keep in our pockets. At the very least it gave me a script to work with.

On Sunday, I drove into the little lakeside neighborhood alone. Erin was going to meet me at the open house. At first glance, the area seemed pretty quiet—so quiet that after driving past the first few homes, most of which were quaint cottages that were obviously just summer homes, I wondered if I was in the right area. It was a nice enough neighborhood overlooking the lake, but I had expected to see vacant lots and large, half-constructed homes.

As I drove farther along the coast, I came to a road that led to a long dock flanked on each side by a sandy beach. Directly across the street from the dock was a skeleton of a three-story home, and next to that was a vacant lot where a home used to be. I looked further up the street and saw a series of "For Sale" signs. I don't think I had ever seen so many in one place at the same time. It seemed odd.

I finally found the open house; it was being held in a small cottage. Erin's car was parked with the mish-mash of cars skirting the road—family cars and old beaters like mine intermingling with Mercedes, Bentleys, and BMWs. I was ready to meet our next upscale customer.

Once inside, a quick look around told me why people were buying these properties and tearing the houses down to build new ones. The cottage was rustic with small, scattered windows that didn't provide much of a view; there was no insulation and no heating other than the fireplace, and the electrical wiring looked like it could be out of date. It certainly wouldn't make a comfortable year-round home.

I found my way to the living room, where all the mingling was happening. There seemed to be people from all walks of life; some looked like they just returned from a hunting trip while others looked like they were from some financial firm in Boston. After meeting Chris Corro, I knew the clothes didn't make the man, so I tried not to hold on to any first impressions.

After a few minutes of sizing up the crowd, I heard the clicking of high heels on the hardwood floor. I turned to see Erin, dressed in a tight black party dress. She smiled at me. "Hey, Jack! Have you tried the deviled eggs? They're delectable!"

"No, I just got here," I said. "Besides, I didn't really come here to eat. We're trying to drum up business, remember?"

"Oh yeah, for sure, but hey, might as well have a good time doing it!" She winked at me. "Anyways, I got here about thirty minutes ago, and I sort of got my bearings. I can bring you up to speed if you like."

"Please. You know, if the cars outside are any indication, then we have some good prospects."

"You bet. So, it seems to me like there are two primary camps here: about seventy percent of the people here are looking to buy the cottage for what it is while thirty percent would tear it down and start from scratch. Those who want to level this place are definitely wealthier; many of them work in Boston, but there are some from as far away as Los Angeles."

"What do you know about the seventy percent?"

"Most of them are looking for weekend or holiday homes," said Erin.

"You mean summer homes?"

"No. It turns out that the ski resort at the mountain nearby had a change in ownership in recent years. Apparently it went from being a subpar ski mountain to being one of the top resorts in New Hampshire. Since that turnover, the lake hasn't been the only attraction—the mountain has become one as well."

"But there's no way anyone could live in this house during the winter," I said. "I mean, look around—there's no heating or insulation. Perhaps we could find people interested in renovation as well."

"Yes, I thought the same thing." Erin discreetly pointed to a man in the corner wearing paint-stained jeans. "Turns out, we're not the only ones."

"What do you mean?"

"That guy is a local carpenter. He has been renovating homes all over this area and specializes in turning summer cottages into all-season homes. And from what I've gathered from his website, he does it fairly cheaply as well." Erin pulled out her phone and pointed to his web page. I skimmed through it.

"Well, he shouldn't be too much of a threat," I said. "We're in totally different specializations. If someone buys this home and wants to rebuild, I don't think he would be up for the job. Just read his testimonials—not a single rebuild or full construction project, just renovations."

"I hope you're right," said Erin. "Anyways, I think I have a clue as to which of these people are the most likely to buy." Erin nodded her head at a man and a woman talking in the center of the room. "Those two have bought several properties in the area. The woman has bought something like ten properties and converted them into upscale rental homes, which she frequently lends out to the family. The gentleman has done the same, for the most part, except he is only renting his homes out during the winter."

"Just for the winter?"

"Yup. He invites scores of friends and family up during the summer, so he doesn't bother renting them out at that time."

"Any other contenders to be aware of?"

"There's a couple looking to turn this place into a vacation home. The local carpenter has already spoken with them and from what I overheard they are more interested in a relatively cheap renovation, so I don't think we should bother with them. I think those are the three main people interested. I'll see if I can get the attention of the lady and the gentleman."

"I'll go meet some other people," I said. "Even if they aren't interested in this house they might be looking at others in the area. They might even have other projects for us."

"Sounds good—see you in a bit," Erin said as she rushed off, grabbing a glass of champagne from the counter before sliding into the middle of the gentleman's and lady's conversation. I watched her in action. She seemed to be a natural social butterfly. The three of them were soon laughing and having a good time. Whatever the conversation, I only hoped she'd remember also to talk business. In some ways I wished I had that natural ability to keep people entertained and happy. In order to help Jack's grow, I wondered if I would have to develop that skill too.

I finally motivated myself to move around the crowded room. For the next few hours I eavesdropped on conversations, and when I found the right people, made myself available. After a while, I learned that most of the people, who wanted to totally rebuild the homes had not yet thought about whom they'd hire to do it. Fortunately, or unfortunately, they had never heard of Jack's Modern Design. When I told them about us and mentioned a few of our projects most people listened politely, but I could tell I was not connecting—until I mentioned Chris Corro.

One man in particular, William, nearly spit out his drink when he heard the name. It turns out that he and Chris hung out together at a nearby golf club. Will had heard about our housing project from Chris and was looking for a carpentry group that did work like ours, but he had only looked in the local area. He was thrilled to hear that we were willing to come out this far. He told me about one property he was buying that would need new construction, so we exchanged details, and he asked me to stop by later that month to check things out. We set a date and time.

I was ecstatic! A new project! Even though it wasn't set in stone, at least, we had a chance to land the deal.

I poked around a bit more and gave my information to a few others. I was surprised by how keen people were about my work. It sure provided a much-needed boost to my self-confidence.

As the open house ended, I looked around for Erin. I saw her sitting on the dock. I started to get a bit irritated, feeling that perhaps she had forgotten the purpose of our trip. I went across the road to talk to her.

She looked over at me as I approached, then stumbled as she tried to stand. She explained herself, "Hey, Jack, sorry. I just had to sit down for a bit; my feet are *killing* me. I've been standing in these heels for what feels like an eternity."

"It's all right, Erin. How did your conversations go?"

"Great! Thomas, the older gentleman you saw, was a bit flirty at first, which upset Jennifer, the woman. Anyway, I got to tell them about what Jack's Modern Design does, and the Corro project and they took a very keen interest. They both seemed interested in our work. I think Jen will get this particular property because she owns a few in the area and is offering a good ten thousand more than the asking price. She wants us to evaluate the landscape after she levels the property. Thomas would like us to take a look at another property on another lake across the state. It shouldn't be a problem for us since it is about the same driving distance for most of our teams. I think we got the projects you wanted!"

This was great news! We had the potential for three big projects within the next month. Only now I had a different problem—could we handle all three at once? Should I even think of rejecting an upscale, incredibly affluent client? I asked Erin, "How set on using us, was Thomas and Jennifer to do their work?"

"Um . . . pretty set, I'd say. They both had looked for upscale builders in the area but couldn't find anyone who could handle unique designs. They had heard about the Corro house as well as the hotel renovation. In fact, Jennifer worked with the conglomerate that gave us that particular job. So it seems that as long as Jennifer's offer gets accepted, and Thomas is good for his word, we've got the jobs."

"Well, I think we've done our job for today," I said. "Thanks, Erin, for being a terrific help. We can go home."

After Erin had left, I stood there for a while. Three potential jobs! What would I do? We couldn't possibly take on all of them. This was more than I dreamed. It was too much. Everything seemed too good to be true. We had landed three potential scores. Even though none was set in stone, this was the first time I had gone out and actually marketed directly for my business.

I sat down. My mind and emotions jumped back and forth: what fantastic success—this was too good to be true; we had finally made it— all these deals could come through. I wish I learned earlier about how powerful an influence marketing could have; even if only one job came through, Jack's would continue to grow with ease.

# Chapter 14
## ON THE ROAD

A couple weeks had passed since Erin and I had gone to the open house. Even though Erin stayed in contact with Thomas, William, and Jennifer, none of the projects had yet finalized. I felt as though we were spinning our wheels and wouldn't actually land one.

On an off chance, I asked Erin to compose an email describing some of our projects. The hotel we had worked on had finally opened, so we got some photos from its manager. The pictures of the beautifully decorated rooms and the swim-up bar were marvelous. I was truly proud of how it turned out.

Erin took the hotel pictures, some from the Corro house, and a few other images from some smaller projects, and created a lovely email compilation. She also added client testimonials. We sent the email to our three big prospects.

We heard back almost immediately. Jennifer had only recently closed on the house and had just begun demolition. She asked if we could help her design and build her new lakeside home. As good news as that was, it still meant roughly a week of down time for my staff; most of them simply couldn't afford to take that time off. I asked Lisa to pursue one of the smaller projects people had inquired about. She dug up a small renovation project.

Being that the job was so small—two weeks to remodel a few bathrooms—Jack's would make only a few hundred bucks net, maybe a thousand tops. At face value, it seemed like nothing but a time sink, but this would be a good project to do that, and make sure each newly formed team worked well together.

I put Tommy with Kurt's old team and assigned him to do the bathroom renovation project. I had Kurt take on Tommy's team, who would work with me setting up the new housing job. Kurt's team would be Everett, the twins, and our electrician, Carl. These men had been my employees the longest. I was concerned how they might react to the change, so I figured if they worked with me I would be able to see first-hand how well the rearrangement was going. I also thought it'd be good to work closely with Everett on the design plans for the new home. He was now a fully licensed carpenter and, combined with his modeling skills; he was every bit as good as, or even better than any architecture student I had met. I looked forward to working with him on new ideas for the lakeside home project.

I don't know why I felt pessimistic on the day we drove out to meet with Jennifer at her new lakeside plot; I was concerned that the demolition team wouldn't have properly cleaned up after themselves. I didn't want to spend extra time and money cleaning up people's messes.

Kurt, Everett, and I arrived at the site at the same time. Kurt looked confused as he asked me, "Jack, are you sure we're at the right place? It hardly looks like a house was ever here!"

"Yeah," Everett said, "You said the place had a basement; either they cleared out all that concrete perfectly, or they just buried it. Can you imagine us trying to dig out an entire basement full of dirt?"

I tried to picture the home as I had seen it a month earlier. "The ground level is too low for anyone to have just filled in the basement. It looks as though they removed the foundation."

"Well that's good," Kurt said. "That means we've got a lot of leeway in our design."

Everett looked up the road. "Looks like our client has arrived." A black Mercedes SUV pulled in behind Everett's truck.

As Jennifer got out of her SUV, she carried a massive notebook under one arm. She walked towards us. "Hi there, Jack." We shook hands. Her firm grip was intimidating.

"This is Kurt," I said, "one of my managers who will oversee the project when I'm not around."

Kurt extended his hand. "It's a pleasure. I look forward to working here; this is a very pleasant location." They shook hands. I couldn't tell if Jennifer was deliberately exerting herself, as I could see Kurt wince from the strength of her grip.

She looked at him and said, "I would have thought Chris Corro's house would have been in a nicer location. What do you think?"

Kurt chuckled nervously. "Well, yes, his home might have had a better view of the mountain than it does, and he certainly doesn't have a beach, but it is in a very secluded area."

Jennifer's smile reminded me of someone playing poker. Ah, right, I thought, she was testing us to make sure that Kurt and Everett were the same employees who actually built Chris Corro's place. I spoke before she could do the same with Everett. "And this young man is Everett. He helped me design the Corro home. He's an excellent model builder with invaluable insight."

"Great!" she immediately responded. "I look forward to seeing what you can do." She opened her notebook and continued, "Speaking of models, I have something you might like to look at." She pulled out a heavy, folded piece of drafting paper and handed it to me. I opened it to discover an absolutely stunning design. She had created a very detailed floor plan and layout of nearly every aspect of her dream home. She had even included locations for boilers and oil tanks and a generator. I waved Everett over to take a look. Seeing it, his eyes instantly widened.

"Did you come up with all this yourself?" Everett asked. "It is incredibly detailed."

"Not exactly. I borrowed a lot of the design from a friend who lives near Lake Tahoe. The plan's not entirely the same because his house was built more into a hillside. I had to flatten the design to make it work with this lot. I also added something that requires your specific skills." As she pointed something out on the plan, I saw Everett's eyes grow big and round.

"You are trying to make a deck that is nearly fifty feet long! And thirty feet of that is over the water! And a secondary deck above that!"

"Hold on—is that even legal?" Kurt chimed in.

"Yes, it is," Jennifer said confidently, "as long as there are no structures directly *in* the water, including support structures. I have rights to extend roughly thirty feet over the water, which gives your crew about twenty feet on land where you can place any necessary supports. My question is, can you do it?"

I scanned over the blueprints; I had some inclination as to what we might be able to do. As I was about to speak, a thought flashed through my mind: *challenge your employees.* "Everett, what are your thoughts?"

Everett, seemingly caught off guard, began to think out loud, "Hmm. It certainly is doable. But twenty feet of supports won't easily bear the weight of such a structure unless we use titanium alloy, which would be ridiculously expensive—in the realm of one hundred grand, I'd guess. But, I don't think that's necessarily the way to go. Better yet, we might be able to use the same support system we used at the Corro house, coupled with a suspension-like setup tied to the second-floor deck, might work quite nicely."

"So that's a 'yes'?" Jennifer asked.

"A tentative yes," said Everett. "I need to create a model and do a bit of research on what we can use for suspension that doesn't look hideous. The last thing you want is a bunch of cables running up the length of your house."

I added, "Perhaps we could add stairways down from the upper deck to the lower deck on either side. We could conceal cables by running them under each stairway. They'd hardly affect the view."

"That would help massively with the supports and conceal them too," Everett said. "But let me check the blueprints to make sure everything is viable. I will also discuss this with our consulting structural engineer."

I handed them to him, "Here you go. And why don't you and Kurt check the area to make sure there's nothing left over of the former structure—just in case." Everett nodded and asked Kurt to grab some tools from his truck.

"Your people seem quite competent," Jennifer commented. "I just hope you can deliver."

"No problem there. I'm lucky to have those two. It's usually not a question for them of whether or not they *can* do the job, rather, it's *how*."

"Good to hear that . . ." she trailed off. "One more thing. Remember Thomas, the man who with me during the open house? He is a business partner and long-time friend and he wanted me to ask you about a job he has in mind."

"Oh? I hadn't heard from him since the open house. I was beginning to wonder whether or not he had any projects."

"Yes, he does, but he has been in Tokyo on a business trip and had misplaced your business card. He wanted me to ask you if you have built any barns."

"Barns, huh? I have personally worked on a few barns in the past. My mother used to do quite a bit of horseback riding, and I'm very familiar with them."

"That's good to hear, Jack. Thomas has some horses that he loves to death, and he is looking to build a fairly sizeable barn for them. More importantly, he wants the barn to be economical, even self-sustaining if possible; heating and cooling such a large space takes massive amounts of power. He is big on ecology and energy conservation, so the more you could do on that end would be important to him."

"Aside from the obvious solar panels," I said, "and proper insulation and such, I might have to do a bit of research, but I'm sure we can make it happen."

"That's great. I think Thomas is getting back in the next two weeks. He will probably want to meet with you personally and go over some details." Jennifer's phone rang. She turned to talk, then turned back to me. "I'm sorry, Jack. I've got to go. It was good to meet you, and I'll email Thomas that your guys are good to go, and he can meet with you whenever. And let me know when you get that model together and have a material and expense list to show me. I'll take a look and write you a check—if I like it." She winked, then shook my hand and added, "I like what I've seen so far." With a graceful about-face, she turned around and walked to her SUV.

I turned towards Kurt and Everett who were poking into the ground with some stakes; my guess was they were looking for any remnants of the previous basement. I stood there not knowing what more to do. With more potential projects than I had ever envisioned, everything seemed too real. I could visualize Jack's heading to a new level. Even though the current deals weren't entirely solidified, I knew we were on the right track, and I could feel in my heart that everything I ever hoped and dreamed for was within reach.

The next morning I was awakened by my cell phone. "Oh God," I sighed to myself, "If that's my phone, then I'm really late!" I had some work I wanted to do on Everett's model for Jennifer's home. I got up and began to freshen up for the day, but as I proceeded to the bathroom, I noticed it was still dark out. A few moments later, the ringing started up again. I shook off my grogginess and realized it was actually an incoming call. I didn't recognize the number, so I let it go to voice mail. I would check it later; I had a big day ahead. Besides, it was probably just a telemarketer.

When I checked my voicemail later that morning, it turned out that I couldn't have been more wrong. It was William, the very man I had talked with at the same open house where I had also met Jennifer and Thomas. He had received Erin's email about the completion of the Corro house and was very impressed. He briefly outlined a project he was considering and asked if I could talk with him about it in the near future.

I was excited about this new prospect. Even if Thomas's barn project fell through, it meant that Jack's would still be able to keep busy and profitable. My only concern was whether these jobs would conflict with one another. I wasn't in the position at this moment to hire an entirely new team, but if jobs this large and this profitable kept rolling in, potentially I could.

On Monday, I called William. He described his project. It was a fairly large-scale renovation for a midsized bed & breakfast he owned in the mountains nearby. He wanted to maintain its rustic appearance while also incorporating both modern and elegant design. Although each detail sounded easy enough to handle, the project itself would be complex to manage. I knew we could do it, though.

But now I worried that we actually might end up with all three projects!

Soon enough, my suspicions were confirmed. After a week of planning and discussion, I wound up having three separate projects, with schedules that conflicted. Despite my best efforts to find a way to work all three projects with my existing staff, I would have to outsource much of the work. This meant that my teams would have to work side by side with non-specialized carpenters. Although many of my guys weren't specialized by trade, after working with me for almost a year, they had become quite skilled.

I was concerned about how some of my staff would react, but I was more concerned about who would oversee my outsourced labor. Only one name came to mind: Everett. Even though he was young and still had much to learn, Everett had vision, and, more importantly, he had passion. Passion for his work. Passion for his models. Passion for Jack's Modern Design.

I outlined how Jack's could pull off so many jobs simultaneously. Everything had to be thought out in advance. It all seemed so simple written out—a pen and paper could write destiny, it seemed. Troubles could certainly crop up; but once planned and accounted for, everything was manageable. I went ahead with training Everett in the basics of management.

After a bit of work and a lot of practice, Everett finally made it as a manager. His modeling prowess made him more than ideal to lead teams, and he could think in unique ways, different from Tommy or Kurt. Most importantly, he knew when to ask for help. I chose to test him with Tommy's minor project; he proved himself well. When William's project came to the fore, I found a local contractor who would save my men from doing the more tedious hammer-and-nail work.

Eventually, I had Everett supervise the outsourced carpenters while Kurt and Tommy oversaw the rest of the specialized divisions. With the teams in place and everyone working towards a single goal, everything was set in motion. Our latest projects would bring enough profit for

Jack's so that I could finally take some time off. I might even have time to take a class or two in architecture.

Over time, with Jack's solidly in the black and Erin rounding up potential prospects, the future seemed more secure. Although I couldn't distance myself from the business the way Vern could, at least, I could take some time off every now and then. I did, in fact, take many architecture classes in my spare time, which gave me the knowledge to come up with ideas for our new projects. I even paid for Everett to take few classes in architecture as well. Everett's studies took him to a new level of creativity, and he became my right-hand man.

With things going so well, Erica and I decided to start a family. We agreed that if our first child were a boy, we would name him Vernon, in honor of my mentor who had made possible the success we were now living.

Within a short time, we added "consultancy" to the services Jack's Modern Design offered. With Everett and I having design insight, we could spend some time offering our skills to projects that didn't need the specialized attention of my teams. As far as I was concerned, it was a new product we could offer that took very little time and energy. Even though it didn't bring in the big bucks, it was more than worth it.

Jack's still wasn't fully autonomous; I still had to be there, but I had the free time I always wanted. Erica and I had enough time and money to raise a family; I could take a breather from work once and a while, and, as icing on the cake, I could finally pursue my degree.

The months passed quickly as the company worked diligently on three of the largest jobs in our history. There were hurdles we encountered, as well as some setbacks, but every day when I worked, I felt satisfied and fulfilled by how things were coming together.

One day, I arrived home after a short workday and got out of my car.

Walking into my home, I saw Erica sitting in the family room; she was smiling and laughing. A man with gray hair was seated in a chair opposite her with his back towards me. I looked at the chair next to him. Resting on the cushion was the familiar feathered fedora.

"Vern!" I exclaimed.

He stood up and turned towards me. "Jack, it's good to see you again."

"Vern! What the heck! I thought you were away, caring for the twins? I haven't heard from you in almost a year! What happened?"

"A lot's happened, Jack. The twins had some health issues, but now they're both happy and healthy."

"I can't tell you how grateful I am to see you, Vern."

"I hope things are going well at the company," he said.

"They are, Vern, thanks for your advice. I still wish you had been here, though, because we certainly had our share of difficult times. But, after many painful lessons, I seem to have figured things out. "

"Sounds like we have a lot of catching up to do. Go ahead, tell me what's happened."

"Well, I realized there was a lot you taught me that I wasn't doing. First off, I wasn't good at planning for the future, to clarifying my vision. Looking back, I would say this was my biggest liability. I never stood back and outlined the future; I assumed I could get by just looking a few weeks ahead. This led to some poor choices in hiring, in job choices resulting in the loss of money, the loss of time, and even the loss faith of my employees."

"And now what do you do?"

"I've been keeping my long-term goals written up, particularly focusing on my hiring and marketing processes. Despite having as many jobs as my teams can handle, we still keep hunting for more. I have even developed a separate product of sorts, Everett and I have consulted on a few jobs."

"That sounds creative. How did you choose to develop that product?"

"It cropped up after Everett and I took a few architecture courses together. I realized that Jack's specialized construction teams weren't necessary for every single project. Even though I believe my teams are far more efficient and productive than most carpentry groups, I decided to see if I could sell my skills and my vision as well."

"Excellent. Sometimes adding a new product can be difficult, but it sounds like you've found success with it. How is the business itself?"

"Money is rolling in quite steadily, and our jobs keep us busy. Keeping a focus on innovation is sometimes difficult, but my team contributes ideas very well. It has been eye-opening for me to see that when the staff feels that their opinions matter, they then bring their all to the table, including their minds."

"That's right, isn't it?" he said. "For most people, when they feel they can grow in their environments, they'll often amaze you. Congratulations for discovering that on your own! And where are you relative to reaching your final goal?"

Erica stood up and said, "If you'll excuse me, I need to start dinner. Perhaps you'd like to continue your conversation on the deck."

"Sure, hon," I said. "OK with you, Vern, if we talk on the deck?"

"Of course."

We went outside and relaxed in the evening air. I continued with my story, "So, toward my final goal—a nearly autonomous business—I still have a long way to go, but it is my three-year goal, and it has only been a year since I've actually been on the right track. Jack's Modern Design still needs me, so I can't take very much time off, but I have enough time to take courses and raise a family. I tell you, Vern, it's like a dream come true."

"Excellent! Many business owners would be jealous of that potential, let alone what you've already accomplished." He looked up at the setting sun, drawing my attention to it as well. The red and orange sky was phenomenal.

I searched for words to thank him, "There's still a lot to be done, I know, and it might take time, but my ultimate goal is within reach. You showed me how, Vern, and I know I can do it."

I watched him as he basked, eyes closed, in the orange glow of the setting sun. He turned his head toward me. He looked straight at me and said, "Jack, I'm proud of you."

That was all I needed to hear.

# ABOUT THE AUTHOR

David Hilton, MBA, M.Ed., started out working in his family's "mom & pop" business, and soon realized that the business wasn't fulfilling his dreams, yet he saw potential for growth in that business. Over the next thirty-five years and many struggles he grew the company to a multi-location, multi-million-dollar business where he recruited, hired, and trained over 500 people.

As a business advisor and CEO coach he has helped more than 250 other business owners reach significant success in their businesses. More important than the financial wealth he has helped owners create is the freedom he has helped them gain to enjoy their lives apart from their businesses.

For additional information, please visit:

**www.MySparkBook.com /resources**

CPSIA information can be obtained
at www.ICGtesting.com
Printed in the USA
LVOW08*2041131116

512779LV00008BA/55/P

9 781630 479497